"While reading Gene Burkart's *Bearing Witness*, I was reminded of the old Hans Christian Andersen tale, "The Emperor's New Clothes." Like that little child, Gene Burkart cultivated the habit of telling the truth. The essays in *Bearing Witness* expose one contemporary certainty after another for what they are: illusions, deceptions, swindles. Do children really need more school in order to grow up? Is an economy devoted to perpetual growth healthy for human communities and the natural world? Is there only one way of doing politics, one that privileges the rich and undermines local communities?"

—Daniel Grego, Executive Director, Milwaukee Transcenter for Youth

"Gene's essays are a string of pearls—lustrous, compact, and beautiful. Each is filled with that rarest of gems in a virtual world: common sense. To read his words is to know the mind of a great man, and the spirit of a great friend. Friendship was the focus for his thought connecting love, gifts and fallibility. To read Bearing Witness is to often remember and frequently learn almost everything important about living a life."

—John McKnight, author of *The Abundant Community: Awakening the Power of Families and Neighborhoods*

"These essays are so quietly compelling that I read the whole collection straight through in one sitting. Gene takes no aspect of modern life for granted—war, poverty, prisons, schooling— and his critiques are hard-hitting. But in the end his words didn't leave me in despair. On the contrary, I'm buoyed by his celebration of ordinary ingenuity and connection. As Gene demonstrates with his plain eloquence, these are the human capacities that may yet save us."

—Susannah Sheffer, author of *Fighting for Their Lives: Inside the Experience of Capital Defense Attorneys*

"Gene was a deeply spiritual person, a homeschooling father, gardener, political activist, writer, philosopher, and a lawyer who fought for the little guy. I'm so glad we have Gene's parables, not only to help us navigate the currents of modern life, but also as a reminder about what a down-to-earth friend and thinker he was."
—Patrick Farenga, co-author of *Teach Your Own: The John Holt Book of Homeschooling*

"In these essays, we encounter Gene, the quiet, upright man, attempting to live a practical philosopher's life in the daily life of his community. I will cherish this brilliant and moving volume as I cherished Gene's friendship."
—David Schwartz, author of *Who Cares?: Rediscovering Community*

BEARING WITNESS

BEARING WITNESS

*Radical Thoughts
on Community,
Politics, Faith, and
Friendship*

Hemlock Press

Originally published as *Bearing Witness: Selected Writings of Eugene J. Burkart,* BackPages Press, 2014.

Design by Patrick Farenga
Cover photo by Sue Burkart of Gene Burkart in front of the MA State House speaking on behalf of prisoner's rights.

ISBN–13: 978-1537002286

ISBN–10: 1537002287

Printed in the United States of America

Hemlock Press, 6 Hemlock Terrace, Waltham, MA 02452

You can order additional copies of this book at www.amazon.com.

*For Dave, Dan, David, and Dominic Burkart
and in memory of mentors and friends
Ivan Illich and Lee Hoinacki*

Acknowledgments

This book would not have been possible without the editorial assistance of Alex Greene, Aaron Falbel, Jennifer Rose, Robin Beaudoin, Dan Melnechuk, and Patrick Farenga. Many, many thanks.

CONTENTS

INTRODUCTION

The volume you are holding in your hands is an absolute gem. For those of you who knew Eugene Burkart—"Gene" to friends and family—this will come as no surprise. For those encountering Gene's writing for the first time, you are in for a treat.

By day, Gene was an attorney who practiced law in his adopted hometown of Waltham, Massachusetts. Being fluent in Spanish, Gene was especially helpful to his numerous Spanish-speaking clients, many of them Guatemalan immigrants. He took on cases involving family law, workplace injuries and accidents, contract and housing law, criminal matters, and he also defended homeschooling families when their right to teach their own children was questioned by overzealous superintendents and school districts.

However, Gene's legal practice occupied only a portion of his vast and prodigious intellect. By night, he was an independent scholar and social critic, an intellectual of the highest order—as evidenced by the writings in this collection. His brand of scholarship was not connected with any lofty institution of higher learning; it was of a most accessible kind, readable by the average person, or even by an interested teenager.

The title of this book, *Bearing Witness*, necessarily prompts the question, bearing witness to what? To what was Gene bearing witness in these writings and in the various forms of activism (vigils, speak-outs, study groups) in which he took part? The common thread that runs throughout this book is Gene's belief and observation that modern society has washed love out of our lives. By "love," he did not mean romantic love or eros but the type of love signified by the Latin *charitas* (also spelled *caritas*). This is the root of our words "charity" and "caring" and is best typified, according to Gene, by the biblical parable of the Good Samaritan. This type of love is always personal, embodied, face-to-face, and idiosyncratic. It emanates from the heart and also from the gut, as in a "gut feeling." The care of *caritas* can never be bureaucratized, systematized, or institutionalized without perverting it and turning it into something else.

Whether Gene is writing about the economy; ways of doing politics; the folly of war-making; nuclear weapons; the bloated and racist prison system; our worship of experts, science, and progress; the way in which various technologies (computers, photography, video, recorded music, clocks) intrude on true relatedness and unmediated sensory experience...at bottom he is pointing to a failure of love: our inability or unwillingness to truly care for each other.

Gene spells this out quite plainly at the end of the short

piece, aptly titled, "What I Believe Is Simple." He does not mince words:

> The Samaritan was touched by the plight of the Jew and felt called to make a personal response. We in our rich society face barriers to that touch and to that call. The barriers are the result of institutionalization. For every suffering person there is, at least on paper, an institution or agency with trained personnel who are paid to attend to that person. It's their job. The personal response is replaced by an impersonal, institutional response, and as our institutions grow strong, our capacity for hospitality grows weak. Ultimately we are confronted with a temptation the Samaritan did not know: the enticement to be free of the great challenge of living in accordance with the Gospel (p.121).

Gene Burkart bore witness to our reliance on institutions, systems, bureaucratic agencies, and technologies to relieve ourselves of the burden of actually having to care for the person or persons who stand before us. That is, to love our neighbor, which was at the core of his faith and of everything he believed in. Over and over, he asks and examines the question, what are these institutions doing to our hearts and to our ability to love one another?

> How many prisons, how many of these islands of totalitarianism, can a nation sustain without becoming deeply contaminated by them? The spirit of totalitarianism is restless and inventive and does not lie safely contained behind high concrete walls and razor wire (p.95).

The ethic of Hiroshima has deeply penetrated American

society, becoming a prominent one in both the public and private realm. But beware. The belief that the ends justify the means is a more deadly poison than the radioactive fallout from the mushoom cloud. It can make us into frightful mutants far removed from the kinds of persons we were originally created to be. Renounce and reject it with all your strength (p.107).

And what we see is that the God of Abraham, Isaac and Jacob and, later of Mark, Matthew, Luke and John, is principally concerned with how people live. Time and again, people are condemned for their hardness of heart. This is not your conventional morality, for what makes hardness of heart so unsettling is that it causes a blindness such that one cannot see one's own faults. We are all susceptible to it, and there are certain telltale signs of its presences: complacency, self-satisfaction, the love of comfort, prestige or power (p.130-1).

The last essay in this collection, "From the Economy to Friendship: My Years Studying Ivan Illich," deserves special mention. It is the most deeply personal and autobiographical piece Gene ever wrote. He worked long and hard on this essay, and with the sage advice of Illich's own friend and editor, Lee Hoinacki, Gene turned out a masterpiece. I have read this essay more than a dozen times by now, and each time I learn something new and valuable from it. Those who knew Gene well were aware of his fascination (to put it mildly) with the ideas of the philosopher, historian, theologian, and social critic Ivan Illich (1926–2002). Gene's fascination with these ideas was not merely intellectual or academic. Gene read Illich with a purpose: How does one understand the strangeness of modern society? How can one live decently or honorably in it? How can one love one's neighbor through the morass of institutions and systems that get in one's way?

As the title of this concluding essay suggests, Gene came to see that the key was cultivating the art of friendship to a very high degree. Gene, along with his wife Sue, was a virtuoso at this art. I knew Gene for 23 years and he was one of the best friends I ever had. Gene was always a big-hearted guy, but his study of Illich made his big heart grow even bigger. The extent to which, and the seriousness with which, he practiced the art of hospitality is legendary. I would be hard-pressed to think of a more generous soul. As Gene so eloquently put it:

> The more I came to know Illich personally, the more I would see that friendship was the very center of his life and work. While he never wrote an essay or treatise explicitly on the subject, friendship is a theme that consistently appears in his writing, a connecting thread through all his books. I eventually concluded that the best way to understand Illich's work is a detailed study of the myriad and varied barriers to friendship that exist in modern life.... No one I know has seen so deeply as Illich the darkness of our times, no one has examined with such an unflinching eye the enormity of the evil we face. Yet he rests his hope on such a humble, fragile, one might easily say foolish, task: the simple but arduous one of being present to this person who stands in front of me. (p.186)

That, indeed, is the best way to understand Ivan Illich *and* the best way to understand Gene Burkart. The book you are now holding is a catalog of the barriers to the human heart, to *caritas*, that modern society places before us—and how, at least in some cases, those barriers can be overcome. Gene incorporated these ideas into his life and overcame more of these barriers than anyone I have known. Reader, study this slender volume well, for it contains the lessons of a lifetime—the lifetime of one Eugene J. Burkart.

Aaron Falbel
March, 2014

I.

COMMON GOOD

WHAT'S WRONG WITH
THE ECONOMY

Something is wrong with the economy, something graver than the loss of jobs, something more ominous than the near collapse in 2008. What's wrong with the economy can be illustrated by a comparison of two markets: the financial market of Wall Street and the farmers' market of Waltham [Massachusetts].

Wall Street consists of a cluster of glass and steel towers in Manhattan where people work in climate-controlled offices far removed from the ground. Most sit in front of computers, manipulating figures on a screen. Their work causes vast amounts of money to circulate throughout the world. For all its complexity and sophistication, the work is basically very simple. It's a form of speculation—gambling, really. One spends money today hoping to get more tomorrow.

The farmers' market is located in the parking lot at the corner of Moody Street and Main Street. On Saturdays from June to October vendors set up tents and display the goods which they have grown, raised, or made: fresh fruits and vegetables, flowers, organic meats, cheese, eggs, bread, honey, soap, artwork, and handicrafts. Money is spent at this market in order to take home something good to eat or enjoyable to use.

Two markets: One is run by giant corporations operating on a global scale, the other by small family businesses that are locally rooted. While both are called markets, they have little in common. They are governed by very different rules.

What drives the corporations on Wall Street, as well as the other transnational corporations of the global economy, is one thing and one thing only—profits.

The nature of their markets requires that all other considerations be swept away. Employees are expendable, no matter how many years of devoted service. Customers are an anonymous mass to be manipulated by clever advertising. Products are whatever sells, regardless of whether they are useful or necessary. Land, water, and air are mere resources to be exploited in the production process. Even patriotism counts for little—plant closings at home and tax havens abroad are business as usual.

Furthermore, because of their enormous size, these corporations are "too big to fail." If they are in trouble, the government must bail them out, or run the risk of total economic breakdown.

Markets are human constructs. When they are of a proper scale and proportion, markets serve society. When they become too big and powerful, however, a transformation occurs: society itself becomes subordinate and subservient to markets. What's wrong with our economy is that for some time now corporate markets have dominated and ruled our economic, social, and political lives. But it doesn't have to be this way. There are many other possibilities. Just go down to the Waltham Farmers' Market and let your imagination go to work.

THE LESSON
OF THOMPSON PARK

A t the beginning of the summer of 1986, the neighbor-hood park on Charles Street, Thompson Park, was in bad shape. Everything about it spoke of neglect and blight. Weeds were growing up through the pavement. Litter was strewn about and uncollected, and graffiti covered just about everything. The park had a bad reputation also. It was said that drug dealing took place there, even in the daytime.

The state of the park reflected the wider condition of the neighborhood. Directly across from the park were three old, run-down apartment buildings. One had been boarded up due to a fire suspected to be arson. Graffiti covered the front porches of all three, emphasizing their lack of upkeep.

If someone from a social-services agency had walked through the area at that time, he or she might have been tempted to use a tool of the trade: the needs survey. A list would be drawn up of what people needed: for example, better parks and recreation services, better police protec-tion, perhaps after-school programs for the kids, job training for adults, and so forth. The needs survey looks at people

13

in terms of what they lack. It gives a picture of   people as deficient in some way.

A small group of local residents, however, took another approach. They looked at people for what they had, at their talents and strengths, even if unused or underutilized. Instead of a needs survey, they wanted something else, a celebration. They wanted to hold the first public Hispanic festival in the city and they wanted to do it in the park.

The park, of course, would need to be cleaned up. The organizers approached the young men who had done all the graffiti and asked them for their help. They readily agreed. The new mayor, Bill Stanley, gave his approval and offered to provide paint and brushes to the group. The cleanup soon began.

Over the ensuing weeks, people of all ages from the neighborhood could be seen fixing up the park: pulling up weeds, sweeping the grounds, collecting and carting off trash and litter, and painting. There are a lot of walls in the park, and a lot of painting needed to be done.

First, a thick coat of white paint was brushed onto everything. Then a mural was painted on the back wall, depicting a Puerto Rican flag along with a tropical island scene.

On a lower wall, flags from the nations of origin of local residents were painted. When it was all done, the park looked completely rejuvenated.

On the day of the festival, traditional foods were served which had been prepared in the neighborhood. Music was provided by a group that played at the Spanish

Mass at St. Mary's Church. There was much dancing and singing and the festival was a big success.

It's now 26 years since the festival. The park never again would face the problems of neglect and graffiti it did back then. The festivals became a yearly event, growing so big that they had to move them from the park to the Waltham Common.

I believe that there is an important lesson to be learned from Thompson Park. Social problems today are typically viewed as something to be solved by either the government or the free market, depending on whether one is a liberal or a conservative. The neighbors of Thompson Park, however, had a different approach.

They did not rely on either the government or the market. They themselves (not some expert) defined what the problem was. They came up with a solution and they carried it out, working co-operatively with each other for the common good, not individual advancement.

Government and the market might be of assistance to this alternative way, but their roles are secondary. Furthermore, as governments go deeper into debt and markets become erratic and manipulated by a few, this third way may be our best hope for dealing with the social problems that besiege us.

WALTHAM IS ONE
OF THE BEST

Waltham is one of 746 cities in the nation with a population between 50,000 and 300,000 people. In 2010 *Money Magazine* did an evaluation of these cities in order to rank the 100 best moderately sized cities in America.

The results were published in the August 20, 2010, issue. You may be surprised to hear this, but not only was Waltham one of only four Massachusetts cities included in the top 100, but it also had a high ranking, 36th overall.

Usually I don't place much weight on magazine listings of the "best," but I must admit I was very pleased and proud to see our city in this ranking. Waltham does have a lot going for it and it was good to see some recognition of this.

I was interested to read in the article the criteria the magazine used in its evaluation. Many were what you'd expect but there was one exception that really surprised me.

The usual factors were those you hear about the most: housing affordability, school quality, job opportunities, safety, arts and leisure, health care, ethnic diversity, traffic, parks, gathering places, and community spirit.

What I didn't expect and what seemed so unusual was that cities were excluded from the list if their median income exceeded the state median income by 200 percent. In other words, some cities just had too much money. This was especially surprising coming from a publication called *Money Magazine*, but it was, I believe, a wise decision to do so. It reminded me of a drive I once took through one of our wealthier neighboring towns one early evening.

I recall being impressed with the houses. They were all very big, of interesting architectural style and impeccably maintained. The lawns were perfect too—no weeds, very green, no brown spots.

But after a while, it dawned on me that there was something very strange about this. It was a beautiful spring day at a time when children would be home from school, parents would be home from work and dinner would have been eaten. What was odd was I didn't see any people. The streets were entirely empty.

I did not see children playing hopscotch or jumping rope on the sidewalks. There were no teenagers bent under car hoods tinkering with motors. No basketball games in driveways. No one tending a big vegetable garden. No one sitting on a front porch talking with neighbors out for a stroll. The neighborhoods were devoid of life. They were dead.

Yes, too much money can be a bad thing. It can create places rich in things and paid services, but lacking in the life that makes cities good places to live in. Good cities have a vitality that centers on doing, not having. They are rich in autonomous activities, neighborly initiative and trust, and informal, local ties. Isn't this what we desire and enjoy from living in Waltham?

THE SECOND ECONOMY

There are two economies at work in society, although only one is usually recognized and acknowledged.

The economy everybody knows and is worried about, of course, is the formal economy of the market, where goods and services are produced and consumed in exchange for money. This economy could be called the money economy.

The other economy is mostly hidden and few think of it as an economy. But it's there if you know where to look. This is the informal economy of family, friends, neighbors and community. In this economy people make, do, and care for themselves and each other without money changing hands. This economy is the relational economy.

The money economy is based on contract, impersonal relations, and the bottom line. The relational economy is grounded in trust, personal loyalty and care.

Through much of history the relational economy was the primary economy with the money economy being secondary, serving as an aid or support to it. You see this in the origins of the word *economy*. It comes from a Greek word, *oikonomia*, which means "household management." When Aristotle wrote about the economy, he emphasized self-sufficiency and reciprocity, two of the main characteristics of the relational economy.

Much of the most important work used to be done in the relational economy. Things were made and houses built. Children were raised and elderly cared for. The sick and dying were tended to. Neighborhoods were looked after and protected. Disputes were resolved. Counsel was given, and teaching and learning occurred naturally. Food was grown. Meals were prepared from scratch and eaten at a gathering around the dinner table. Music was made and songs sung.

Things, of course, have changed very much today. Now it is developers who build houses and things are made in China. Police protect neighborhoods and disputes are taken to court. Children are raised by preschool, day care, school and mass media. The elderly are in nursing homes. The sick and dying are surrounded by strangers in medical centers. Food comes from agri-business and people eat convenience foods on the run. Friends and family are scattered hither and yon, and many don't know their neighbors. People sit alone in front of their home entertainment centers.

The money economy has grown enormously since World War II. But as this economy grows strong, the relational economy grows weak and withers away. That's because the money economy feeds off of and cannibalizes the relational economy. It seeks to replace all that the relational economy does by substituting commodities, goods and services that are bought and sold.

But now the money economy is beginning to falter and shake, in this country as well as throughout the world. It is becoming increasingly clear how vulnerable and insecure individuals and whole nations can be that depend too much on the money economy. This could be a sign of hope.

NOT STIMULATED BY
GOING OUT AND BUYING

President Obama wants everyone to go out shopping and start buying things. It doesn't really matter what we buy, so long as we buy. He and his economic advisers also want banks to lend us money so that we can buy what we don't now have the money for. All this buying, spending and borrowing will be good for the economy, they tell us. It will help restore "consumer confidence" and "stimulate" the economy out of the recession.

I don't really understand much about high level economics. I couldn't tell you what a hedge fund is or a derivatives market or a bundled security. But I do know what debt is. My parents taught me that it is not a good thing. They had learned this from their parents, who learned it from theirs and so on. This venerable way of thinking, however, doesn't seem to have much of a place in the kind of economy we find ourselves in these days. The old rules for living don't apply anymore in this new age, a glorious one according to its promoters, the age of the global economy.

Over time, economic activity has moved from local and regional markets to national and now global markets.

Today the whole world has become one gigantic market. This expansion in the size and scope of markets has resulted in the enormous concentration of economic power in the hands of a few. Some, like Citibank, are so big that, regardless of their egregious conduct, they are "too big to fail." If they were to collapse, the whole global economy might collapse with them.

As power grows and becomes more concentrated for some, independence and self-governance lessens for the rest of us. Increasingly, decisions made by the powerful few in corporate or government boardrooms have a great effect over our lives. Strangers in distant places now decide our economic fate. The advocates of the global economy, however, say that we should not worry. Any loss in freedom or control over our lives is more than made up for with the gains.

The gains, of course, are all those products which fill our stores or fill our gas tanks. From the far corners of the world, stuff of all kinds flows into our country in ever greater quantities and cheaper prices. What more could we want? The global economy promises to be the one, true path into the brilliant future that awaits us: the consumer paradise of unlimited abundance, of more, more, more.

What we are witnessing, however, is nothing less than the replacement of the democratic ethos with a consumer ethos. The moral bankruptcy of this shift is matched by financial bankruptcy: Unprecedented trade imbalances, budget deficits, national debt and personal debt.

Stimulating the economy will not get us out of this

mess. It's time to forge a different way entirely. We would do well to begin by drawing on the wisdom of our ancestors, those who knew what was enough and what was too much, who respected natural limits and exercised self-restraint, who knew that what is most important in life is not material possession or financial security, who valued freedom over comfort and wealth.

GROWTH RATE MOVING UP
NOT A NECESSITY

E conomics has its dogmas just as much as religion does. But while religious beliefs have been subject to widespread questioning and doubt in our skeptical age, the doctrines of economics are largely treated as unassailable truth. They are taken as gospel, so to speak.

One of the cardinal tenets of economic orthodoxy is the belief in the necessity and goodness of economic growth. Economic high priests of otherwise differing economic faiths—capitalist, socialist, communist—are all in agreement on this one dogma. They believe that the health of any given economy is measured by its growth rate. A high growth rate is considered a good thing, while a low rate or no growth, is a cause of grave concern.

What this means in tangible terms is that every year the total dollar amount of goods and services produced and consumed must increase. At a little above a 7 percent growth rate, for example, people would be consuming twice the goods and services in 10 years' time as before. According to the logic of economics, people then would be twice as well off.

The growth doctrine, however, is fundamentally flawed. It simply does not fit with reality. First, it proposes the unlimited, infinite expansion of economic activity in a limited, finite world. The earth has only so much natural wealth to give and can absorb only so much poison and pollution. If the rest of the world were to deplete and pollute at the rate of the American consumer, there would not be much earth left that was habitable.

Secondly, the available evidence shows that beyond a certain point growth does not promote social well-being but rather its opposite, social decay. The U.S. economy has grown enormously over the past five decades, but instead of greater satisfaction, we find growth of a different, troubling kind: in levels of divorce, abortion, one-parent families, incarceration, police presence, drug use (legal and illegal), mental illness and depression, obesity, violent and pornographic entertainment, and corruption in business and politics.

Just as economic growth damages the natural world, so too does it harm the social order. This should not surprise us. How could something that is so harmful to nature not also be harmful to society?

Perhaps it's time to once again observe the lilies of the field. They neither toil nor spin, but most instructively for us, they also know when to stop growing. They never grow to be too big.

WHAT IS DOWNTOWN
REVITALIZATION?

I'll never forget the remarks made by a waitress at the Heritage Restaurant about a week before it closed its doors forever in 2001.

The Heritage was a small restaurant on Moody Street that had been open for business for over four decades. It served only breakfast and lunch, and had a strong local clientele.

The waitress had grown up in Waltham. She had worked for the Heritage as a teenager. Later she left the city for a while, but upon her return she got her old job back. She was probably in her early thirties by then.

Speaking with some emotion in her voice, she told us what the closing of the Heritage meant to her. "My first job was at this restaurant. I grew up here. I know just about everyone who comes in now. It's like a family to me."

The Heritage had that effect on its customers as well. It may not have been a place "where everybody knows your name," but it came close. If you came by regularly enough, you'd get to be known. It was, therefore, not just a place to get food, but also a place to have an informal social life.

Much important business happened at the Heritage. The news of the neighborhood was passed around. A ride might be arranged for someone. A tip on a job might get handed on. It all centered on conversation, which, whether serious or playful, was always lively and enjoyable. And hardly anyone was excluded. I can remember seeing on a number of occasions someone who was going through hard times sitting and chatting at the Heritage for hours, all for the cost of a cup of coffee.

In my last column, I distinguished the money economy from the relational economy. I pointed out how in earlier times the money economy served to strengthen and support the relational economy, but that that has largely changed. The money economy now operates to dismantle and replace the relational economy. There are still, however, remnants left of the older economy and the Heritage was one of those places.

Currently, much attention has been given to downtown revitalization. A citizens' committee has been formed. The mayor's office and City Council have shown interest. Even Bentley University has commissioned and completed an in-depth study on the issue. Nowhere in the discussions or in the report, however, have I seen any appreciation for the kind of business the Heritage represents.

Instead, merchantability is given precedence over sociability. The quick turnover of money and customers seems to be the focus while the leisurely pursuit of stronger relationships in the local community is not mentioned. This is terribly ironic. It has been the shopping malls and big-box stores that have most damaged the downtowns of cities, and it is these kinds of places that are most based upon the money economy and the bottom line.

Ray Oldenburg, in his classic *The Great Good Place,* has shown how important establishments that emphasize sociability have been for the culture of cities throughout history. Athens had its agora and Rome its forum. London brings to mind pubs; Paris, cafés; Vienna, coffee houses; and Munich, beer gardens. Closer to home, colonial America had its taverns.

It was in the taverns of America that the vision of a new kind of society emerged. Perhaps we could draw on this heritage to envision a restored and renewed downtown for Waltham.

THE SPINNING WHEEL
AND THE CLOTHING RACK

*From a speech given at the annual Clothing Exchange
Luncheon in May, 2000*

Good morning, boys and girls, and welcome to your
first day of R.E. Classes at First Parish. We are in a new
room this year, and you've probably noticed the clothing
racks along the back wall. You're probably also wondering
what they are doing there and what they are for. Well, today
our first lesson will be to talk about those racks, for, you
see, to many of us at First Parish they are very important
things that have a lot of meaning for us, and say a lot about
our hopes and dreams. You could say they are a symbol for
us of a better world—one we are striving to build together.

Perhaps the best way to start today would be to first
talk about another symbol that was very important to
a man you studied last year, Mahatma Gandhi. You may
remember that Gandhi was the great leader who helped
free his country, India, from the colonial rule of the
British. He showed the world that armies and guns could be
defeated by people who practiced non-violent resistance.

What many people forget today is that Gandhi was very afraid that after independence India would be no freer than before; that the British rulers would simply be replaced by Indian rulers who would keep things as they were—with the rich, rich and the poor, poor. Gandhi knew that for there to be real change, a different way of life would have to be adopted and for him this way became symbolized by the spinning wheel. As a symbol and also as a real tool, the spinning wheel could lead India into real independence. For Gandhi knew that real freedom would only come if people lived simply, self-sufficiently and cooperatively.

For some of us at First Parish, the clothing racks are similar to Gandhi's spinning wheel. They are a symbol for a better way of life, one that is freer, that is based on simplicity, self-sufficiency and cooperation. Well, probably you are wondering what I mean by this, and it's certainly true that symbols sometimes are hard to understand. Sadly, India and the world still have not understood Gandhi's spinning wheel. Therefore, for the rest of today's class I am going to explain to you in more detail what the clothing racks have to tell us, what lessons we can learn from them. For me, there are four in particular.

First, the clothing racks are used by something called the Clothing Exchange. It's a kind of store that sells used clothes. Now some of you might know that clothing is one of the three basic needs of life. By basic needs, we mean that without them we cannot live. The three basic needs are food, clothing and shelter. Any work that involves the basic needs of living certainly must be very important work, one of the most important works in the society.

But today people are very confused about needs. Many think things are needs that really aren't. They think that they just can't live without certain things which aren't really necessary for their lives. They will spend a big part of their life working very hard to get money to buy things which they think they have to have in order to be happy, and when they get those things they don't become happy but think they need still more things which they then continue to work very hard to get.

Some of you may have heard of people called advertisers. They are the people who make the advertisements you no doubt have seen. Their sole job, and they make a lot of money at it, is to make people believe that something is a basic need—that they couldn't or wouldn't want to live without it—even though it really isn't. They are very good at what they do. So when you look at the clothing racks, it will help you to remember what is a real need and what isn't. This is a very important thing to be able to do in your lives. If you want to lead a good life you must know what's necessary to have and what isn't.

Second, the Clothing Exchange racks hold clothes that have been used. They are not the brand-new clothes you see in other stores; someone has worn these clothes before. But you can see that they are in fine condition; some you can't even tell have been used.

What usually happens when a person has something which he can no longer use or wants? Sometimes it's given to a friend or family member, but you know what usually happens—it gets thrown out. You do have garbage day at your houses and have seen all the trash barrels on your street on garbage day. There are lot of them, aren't there? The barrels keep getting bigger and many houses have more than one. Think of all that trash a city throws out in one day, all that stuff thrown out and not used again. And where does it go? Just because we don't see it any more doesn't mean it disappears. It goes somewhere. Some gets burned up so it goes into the air as smoke and into the ground as ashes. Other stuff just gets buried. Well, we do know that this isn't good for the air or the soil or the water.

There are, however, some people who say that this is all a good thing that we throw stuff out. Because the more we throw away, the more things we will buy to replace them. This creates jobs and is good for the economy. It makes the economy grow, which to some is a very important thing. If we saved things and took care of them the economy would suffer.

The people of the Clothing Exchange, however, say that this is crazy. Their parents taught them to take care of things, to use them well and repair them if necessary. They were taught that to throw things out is not a good idea, it's wasteful, and to be wasteful is a sin. We hope that these clothing racks will be a reminder in your lives to take care of things and not be wasteful. (You will find that this is a very hard thing to do in today's world.)

The third lesson is that if you go the Clothing Exchange you will notice something different and special about it. All the people who work there know each other very well and like each other's company. You will hear laughter and stories told and you'll see people helping each other out. The customers know this and seem to like it. They know that they will see the same faces, people they know, whenever they go and some go often enough that they become known and are called by their own names.

While at one time, this kind of place, a friendly place where people knew one another well, was very common, and most stores, shops and businesses were like this, they are now rarer and rarer. In fact there are very few left. You have probably never been to one. You are used to places like McDonald's or Victory supermarket or Costco, where no one knows you and the workers don't smile and laugh much and don't seem like they are very happy in their work. Can you blame them? But you can go to the Clothing Exchange and perhaps by knowing what such a place is like you will seek out and find others in your life or even help to create one.

And, finally, the last lesson is this: If you go to the Clothing Exchange you will see a lot of activity. People putting up clothes on racks, putting them in bags, tying price tags, making change, answering questions and keeping records. Grownups call this activity "work."

And as you have probably noticed, work is something very important to grownups—they spend a lot of time at what they call work. You have all heard the word *job*? Well, for most grownups work is only work if it is done on something called a job. And a job is a kind of work you do in order to make money. If you don't get paid for what you are doing, most grownups would say you are not really doing work. And they also believe that the more money one can make at a job the more important must be the work being done.

You can learn a lot about the true nature of work from the people at the Clothing Exchange. Really important work has little to do with money and most of the important work done in society is not done by jobs. In fact, the more money spent on work, the more likely the work is not only unimportant, but is even useless, wasteful and harmful. This is something Gandhi well understood.

The people of the Clothing Exchange don't work for money—they are not paid for what they do. They work because they want to. They enjoy what they do, they enjoy the company of their co-workers and customers, and they know what they are doing is important work. For them, work is not something you do for money, but it is a way of life, a way of being useful and attentive to others. For them work is not an exchange but is something very different—it is a gift.

Well, class is almost over now and you've been very patient. I hope you can now see that there is a lot more to these clothing racks than you may have thought when you entered this room. Now I don't expect that you will understand all that I have talked about this morning. The really important lessons in life are only truly learned through living them. But you don't have to learn them alone or without guidance. And people have always known (except, it seems, these days) that some of the best guides in life are the older members of the community. That's why the elders were always the most esteemed members. Well, as you may know, most of the people at the Clothing Exchange are older, and that is why I think you can rely on them as such good guides. They have gone through life's trials and tribulations and in their struggles have gained wisdom and insight which they now have offered to us. It would be a shame if you did not take advantage of this great gift.

II.

WAYS OF DOING POLITICS

WAYS OF DOING POLITICS

I would like to tell you a story—a true story about politics. I and several members members of First Parish were involved in this story, and the Harrington Room at First Parish played an important part in it.

In 1983, thirteen years ago, at election time in Waltham, there appeared on the ballot a referendum question. The question asked whether a road should be permitted to be built through Prospect Hill Park. This road was a proposal of the real estate developer who owns Prospect Hill Executive Office Park, Arthur Nelson. He proposed the road as a means for alleviating traffic congestion that occurred at rush hour when those leaving the office park on that side of Prospect Hill drove into the intersection of Totten Pond Road and the Route 128 entrance ramps. The road would siphon traffic from the office park through Prospect Hill Park and onto Totten Pond Road, thus avoiding the intersection bottleneck at Route 128.

The developer would pay for the road plus improvements to the ski slope in the park worth altogether

$500,000. The mayor thought it was a good idea, so much so that he started to call the plan his plan. The City Council voted 10–1 for the plan. The House of Representatives voted 150–1 in favor. The State Senate unanimously passed it and the Governor approved it. Everyone, it would seem, was in favorite of it.

There was one person, however, at least one, who wasn't. He was a young, idealistic, bright attorney who with great passion fought every step of the way against the plan. His name is David Wilson, who at that time was going out with Nancy Rea, a member of First Parish. They are married now with two children and Nancy's mother is Beth Rea, the church's secretary. David had grown up near the park and felt strongly that the road with traffic of 3,000–4,000 cars passing daily through it would irreparably alter the character of the park; it would encroach upon the park as a nature preserve, and only serve to benefit a few powerful persons, setting a very bad precedent.

David became at times a lone voice battling the road. The press made him out to be somewhat of a fanatic. But there were indications that he wasn't alone, and there were others who agreed with him. Then, when it seemed all was lost, David discovered a statute which provided that where public land was being taken primarily for a private use, upon the petition of 15 resident citizens, the taking could be put on a ballot referendum question. David secured the signatures and the issue was placed on the ballot. There were howls of protest. David was accused of being unfair —but finally the people of Waltham would be able to decide.

At about that time I was approached by Marianne Lynnworth, who asked if I could help out in the effort to stop the road. Those of you who have been approached by Marianne, in that quiet, unassuming way of hers, know how difficult it is to turn her down. Soon I was with Marianne, Nancy, David and others in the Harrington Room planning our strategy in what turned out to be a bitterly fought campaign.

Our opposition was formidable, well financed with powerful backers, including the Chamber of Commerce, the *News Tribune* (the major paper in town) and the various firms located in the office park. Our opponent hired a Boston public relations firm, full-page ads were taken out in the paper, and a mass mailing of a very professional flyer went to all residents in the City.

Our effort was truly a grassroots campaign. We found that many in the city did not like the heavy-handed way that the road plan had been pushed and were concerned for the park. We picked up support from the Waltham Council of Neighborhood Associations (WCONA), the League of Women Voters, Waltham Concerned Citizens and members of civic and church groups. The Weddigs and Saulniers helped, and I remember putting up a sign on Ruth Babineau's lawn, years before I was to meet her in person.

We also received support from an unexpected source. A sympathetic state bureaucrat leaked to us a letter Mr. Nelson had written the mayor a year before, in which he stated that traffic congestion was preventing further development of his property and if it were remedied he had plans to undertake a major building project, almost doubling the size of his office park. This letter contradicted what the road proponents all along had been saying—they denied any link to future development. Unfortunately we got the letter late. On the Sunday morning before the election, I picked it up from the official in a supermarket parking lot in Brookline—very covertly, and it wasn't in the paper until election day, Tuesday.

The night before the election I got a call from Nick Meliones of WCONA. He had been a veteran of many battles against developers, at a time when you just couldn't win these. He congratulated us on a good effort, but conceded that ultimately we had been out-classed and out-gunned. I suspected at that time he was right.

Well, election day came and we all gathered together at City Hall that night to hear the election returns—and lo and behold—we pulled it off, we won—by a narrow margin of 500 votes!

Afterwards, while we were celebrating our victory party someone turned to me and said, "I guess this proves that the system works after all." Well, I have thought of that comment often. Looking back now thirteen years later, I have to conclude that our experience did not so much confirm the fine health of the democratic system as it did that we were just very lucky. But the more I have reflected on our experience, the more it has seemed to me revealing of what is happening in politics today and what is the matter with those politics.

In hindsight, it now appears to me that what was going on in our political campaign was not just a matter of two sides contesting a particular issue. It was an example of two very different ways of doing politics, of experiencing and approaching politics, really displaying two fundamentally different understandings of the nature of politics.

Let me outline what I think these two different contrasting ways were, as I see them represented by the two parties to this conflict.

There are eight major differences:

1. A personal way vs. a mediated way

Our approach was direct and personal. We approached people face to face. We relied on the personal conversations with friends, family, neighbors and civic groups. We wrote our own flyers and personally delivered them ourselves, walking through the city, canvassing.

The other way relied on mass communication systems: the public relations firm, advertising techniques, mass mailing through postal service systems, endorsements from those in power, heavy use of media, in this case the newspaper. The meditated, impersonal approach to politics.

2. The common good vs. private interest

Those in our group did not have any special personal stake in the issue other than a better park which would benefit everyone in the city, which would be, at least in our minds, for the common good.

Clearly some who opposed us hoped to achieve a personal gain in the outcome of the conflict. Private self interest, while one could not say that it motivated all of our opponents, obviously was what drove the major forces in the campaign.

3. Non-ideological vs. ideological ways

We were an odd collection of people: Republicans, Democrats, liberals, conservatives and radicals, environmentalists and those who aren't. What brought people together was a common concern about a specific concrete issue—Prospect Hill Park—not a common belief system. And there was great variety in the reasons why people became involved.

The ideology that united our opponents is perhaps the most prevalent and powerful ideology operating today. It is something I would call economism: the abstract idea that what is good for business is good for the public. What is good for the economy, what creates jobs, is good for society, necessarily. Under this scheme of thinking, all is subsumed under economics and economic categories. You know the popular political adage, "It's the economy, stupid."

4. Money-less politics vs. moneyed politics

Money had little importance in our efforts. We had a total budget of about $500—just enough to buy the posters and pay for copying. We made our own signs. None of us was paid to work. Our politics took us away from our money-making activities.

Money was the heart and soul of our opponents' politics. It is what fueled their campaign—over $30,000 (a lot of money in 1983). Those who worked hardest against us were paid to do so; it was their job. Money also was the message put forth by them: Their campaign slogan was "your vote is worth $500,000." And it was, of course, money which was the bottom line for the road proposal in the first place.

5. *Voluntary association vs. corporation*

We were a voluntary association, an informal group united by a common cause. Power was distributed widely. Everybody was important and could play a role. Natural authority governed—those willing and able, were deferred to. Ours was a participatory democracy in organizational form.

The various groups that opposed us—the businesses, the City, the newspaper—were organized in the corporate form. The corporation is structured in the shape of a pyramid; power resides at the top and radiates downward in directives and orders. It is an extremely efficient and powerful way to organize people for a task—armies have always known this. It is not an organizational form which could be called democratic. This may explain why so often— as happened in our case—seemingly different and even opposed groups, like government, business and media, work together in concert. They are, after all, animals of the same species. They understand each other. To them, the voluntary association is a strange and frightening critter.

6. *Enough vs. more*

We were oriented toward restraint, limitation and

preservation of what we have, a belief in enough, and an appreciation for what is.

The other way of politics looks to more, to a relentless dissatisfaction with what one has, a striving for the ever elusive better, more efficient. It is fundamentally an orientation to expansion and power.

7. Politics as part of life vs. professional politics

We were *amateurs* (the word *amateur* being derived from the Latin word for lover). We practiced politics as a part of our life as active citizens. It was a part of our lives, not our entire lives, and not something separate and distinct from our every day lives.

The other way of politics views politics as a separate sphere of activity run and controlled by professionals who make a living out of it. This is the politics of the expert and those who know more than we do. No room for amateurs here.

8. Rooted politics vs. remote politics

We all lived in Waltham. It was our home, our community. We had roots here. We were a placed group who had knowledge and affection for the land which would be affected by the proposal.

Our major opponents did not live in Waltham. Waltham to them was a place to use: a convenient site for offices close to convenient highways. They had no home here and little if any knowledge of or affection for Prospect Hill Park, other than how it could be exploited for a road.

These then are the differences between two different ways of doing politics as exemplified by our experiences. We know which way is the dominant form of politics today. And I think it is safe to say we know that in the great majority of cases when the two ways are in opposition, the way of our opponent will overwhelmingly prevail. But we must ask which of the ways of doing politics is the authentic, legitimate way—the way in keeping with the democratic tradition that has been handed down to us, the way in keeping with the very nature of democracy. So this then is, I think, our present political dilemma: how can we recover a lost way of doing politics?

TIME FOR A NEW POLITICS

M uch of what goes by the name of politics today can be easily divided into one of two camps, with each camp having a position seemingly opposed to the other.

On one side we have what are called the red states composed of Republicans, conservatives, the right, the Tea Party and Libertarians. To varying degrees, they say the major problem facing the nation is big government. It taxes too much and spends too much. It's inefficient and arrogant. It interferes with free enterprise. It threatens family values and controls too much of our lives.

On the other side are the blue states consisting of Democrats, liberals, the left, the Occupy Wall Street and Green movements. They attribute the nation's ills to big business. It threatens the environment and leads us into war. It exploits its employees and exports jobs. It enriches the few at the expense of the many. It has too much influence on politics.

If history is our guide, however, one thing is certain. No matter who gets elected president and no matter who controls Congress, big business and big government will continue to thrive. Take Ronald Reagan, for example, probably the most famous opponent of big government. Over the course of his eight years in office the federal government actually grew in net size.

So why is this so? I think the most plausible answer is that big business and big government are not as opposed to one another as conventional wisdom seems to imply. Rather they need and depend on one another. Big in one means big in the other.

Basically, they are two sides of the same coin. Look at the men (and now occasionally women) who are at the top of big business and big government. They think and act very much alike. Often they have attended the same elite schools, live in the same exclusive neighborhoods and mix in the same social circles. Many have even simply moved from one side of that coin to the other.

Just as the elites who run big business and big government are similar, so too are their organizations. First, they are both of enormous scale. Some of the giant corporations have budgets and personnel that are larger than those of many national governments. Secondly, they are both similarly organized: in the shape of a pyramid, with power concentrated at the top and radiating down through a strict chain of command and division of labor.

It's a structure designed for a few to control the many.

More and more the decisions that most affect our daily lives are not made by us in the communities where we live. Instead, they are made in boardrooms and government offices in distant places by people who do not know us or have affection for our city.

It's time for change. It's time for a new politics, one that restores power to our communities, the power that big business and big government have taken away.

GROWTH OF GOVERNMENT POWER

All levels of government—federal, state and local—have an innate tendency to grow and expand, to become more powerful, to extend their reach into ever more aspects of our daily lives.

While the growth of government power is a relentless force, it often works quietly in almost imperceptible ways. That's because new expansions of government power usually affect only a few people at first, thereby avoiding the attention and resistance of the majority. Two ordinances recently passed with little discussion and no debate by Waltham's city council and mayor offer good examples of this dynamic of power.

The first ordinance bans all persons who are level 3 on the sex offender registry from living within 500 feet of schools, playgrounds and daycare centers. The second requires grocery stores which display fruit and vegetables outside on sidewalks to have a canopy overhanging their produce.

Neither ordinance makes much sense. There is no empirical evidence showing that where a person lives affects his or her likelihood of re-committing a sex crime.

The ordinance is as irrelevant as one banning persons convicted of bank robbery from living near banks or drunk drivers from living near liquor stores.

The other is similarly nonsensical. Fruits and vegetables grow on farms without canopies, of course, and everyone knows to wash their fruit before eating it.

If these ordinances are not about sense, or even common sense, what then are they really about? In both cases a significant increase in government power over our lives has occurred.

Our city government has declared that it now has authority to decide where people can and cannot live. True, today that power is exercised over a small group of outcasts. But a precedent has been set. Tomorrow it may be used against a different group, and later another, and so on. The very fundamental freedom of choosing where we live can now be encroached upon.

Secondly, if something as trivial as how grocers display their produce can be subject to government control, is there any aspect of our lives, no matter how small and mundane, that cannot be considered a potential target for government management, regulation and control?

A BETTER KIND OF TAX

I agreed with much of what the opponents of the Community Preservation Act said about government and taxes. Governments, whether local, state or federal, do have an innate tendency to grow and expand, to become bigger and more powerful, to demand ever more tax monies from us.

And as a government increases in size and power, it inevitably becomes more unresponsive, wasteful and unaccountable. Beyond a certain point, a government can serve its own ends and not the ends of the people.

I think, however, that the CPA opponents misunderstood what this referendum was really about. They made the mistake of seeing it as just another tax. It is not. It is instead a very different kind of tax, one that represents a reversal of how taxes are currently used and conceptualized.

Most taxes come from above. They are imposed by a particular governmental body which then feeds the gathered tax money into its ever-swelling budget. From there the money gets dispersed in complicated and sundry ways, usually beyond the capabilities of most citizens to follow or decipher. Who gets what, what for, and whether it is well spent, is often impossible to know.

The CPA turns this approach to taxes upside down. Citizens themselves initiate the tax (a modest one), and they determine the specific ends for which the tax money will be used—historic preservation, affordable housing, and open space.

Where and how the tax money is used will be easy for everyone to see and judge. The results will be tangible things (not intangible services), displayed in land and buildings right here in our city. And most importantly, if citizens at some point decide that the tax isn't working or is no longer needed, they have the power to revoke it.

The CPA represents a fundamental change in the way taxation is done—it puts control in the hands of citizens. It could therefore serve as a model for a major tax-reform effort at all levels of government. Wouldn't it be good if a greater percentage of the taxes we do pay were similar in design to the CPA?

I do not see why those who seek to reduce taxes could not find allies with those who wish to assert citizen control over taxes. These could, in my view, be two complementary political initiatives.

THE CONSEQUENCES
OF 'COUNTRY FIRST'

The signs were displayed throughout the auditorium at the Republican National Convention. They were all the same size, with the same colors, and with the same message. Speaker after speaker referred to the message of the signs. The signs read, "Country First."

As I watched the convention on TV, I wondered where this injunction, "Country First," came from. It's not to be found in the Bible, the one text which (if you believe opinion polls) is the major guide for most Americans when it comes to discerning priorities and things which are first.

But the phrase sounded vaguely familiar, although I couldn't quite put my finger on it. Then I remembered. In the 1930's in Germany, a favorite song of the National Socialist Party (the Nazis) was *"Deutschland über alles"* ("Germany over everything"). This startled me. Germany over everything. Germany first, country first, America first, America over everything. The messages were the same!

The German song gave expression to a particularly virulent form of nationalism and militarism which had disastrous consequences. While Germany was defeated in World War II, nationalism and militarism, however, remained very much alive. These demons continue to wander the wide world, always searching for new places to make their home.

It has been said that the greatest trick of the devil is to appear as an angel of light. Nationalism and militarism often insinuate themselves in the glow of tender and warm terms, like freedom, peace, sacrifice, love of country and defense of the weak. But there is a way to see through the deception, to see their brutal ugliness. That's because nationalism and militarism always demand blood, and especially the blood of other people's children.

"Country First"? Let's first ask ourselves how many children have been killed, crippled and disfigured in Iraq, Afghanistan, and now Pakistan, as the result of those who think that country is first.

WORSE THAN TERRORISTS

The greatest threat to freedom in America today is not al Qaeda. The worst al Qaeda can do is kill Americans in a terrorist attack. That would be terrible, of course, but killing people is not the same thing as taking away a nation's freedoms.

Al Qaeda has no power to invade our country, take over our government and impose its rule over us. Al Qaeda has not been able to do that to even the weakest and most vulnerable third world country. The threat to freedom lies elsewhere.

If you look at the countries in the world today which do not have freedom, most have not lost freedom to a foreign power imposing its rule over them. With a few notable exceptions, freedom was not lost to invading armies. More commonly, freedom is lost to forces from within a country itself rather than outside it. Powerful persons within a country's own political, military and industrial establishment take freedom away from their countrymen, always on the pretext that it is for the good of the country.

The tools for denying freedom are well known and

used wherever freedom is lost. These tools are: a powerful secret police force manned with undercover agents and paid informants; an extensive surveillance network unrestrained by citizen oversight; secret prisons where people disappear; the use of torture and the official denial of its use; supreme power in the hands of one man, who, as protector of the people, is above the laws of a legislature; propaganda machinery that incessantly plays on people's fears of attack by an enemy; and finally, the loss of *habeas corpus* and due-process rights.

These tools for the suppression of freedom have been put in place in our country. They are beginning to be used.

If freedom is so threatened, why then is there no public outcry in this the land of the free and home of the brave? Dostoyevsky's Grand Inquisitor suggests a sobering answer. When it comes down to a choice, he tells us, most people crave security and comfort over freedom. The enemies of freedom have always relied on this.

SOMETIMES LESS
IS MORE

Representative Thomas Stanley is in favor of a program which would extend the school day for certain selected grade schools by almost two hours. This makes me wonder. What did young Tom think when he was in the fifth grade and the bell rang at the end of the day? Was it, "Gee, I wish I could stay here another two hours"?

More likely Tom was similar to most kids I knew. We couldn't wait for the doors to open. We were tired of being told what to do and what to think and were itching to engage in activities which we were finally in charge of. We yearned for freedom.

Many adults tend to romanticize their school days, forgetting what their experience was really like. The author John Holt attributes this phenomenon to what he calls "the hidden curriculum of schooling." More than any subject matter, more than the content of what is taught, schools teach above all else the necessity of schools. They instill the belief that only in school does real learning take place, only in school can one grow in knowledge, skill and maturity. This is the main lesson taught by schooling.

Most learn this lesson well. It is to be expected that the longer one stays in a particular institution, whether it be school, the military or prison, the more one's view of what is real and possible is shaped by that institution. One's thinking becomes institutionalized. Because of this, many have an inflated sense of the benefit and effectiveness of schooling. They confuse treatment with results, process with substance. They think that more school means more learning, more growth.

Just the opposite, however, is true. At a certain point schooling becomes counterproductive. It produces the opposite of what it is designed to achieve. Have you ever wondered why education reform is always on the political agenda? It's because prolonged schooling itself actually hinders initiative, stifles creativity, smothers curiosity and deadens the joy of learning.

I know this may sound like heresy, but we need less school, not more.

III.

BEARING WITNESS

IN MEMORY OF
MARTIN LUTHER KING, JR.

Today and tomorrow, throughout this country, there will be many words of praise and adulation for Martin Luther King. It might, therefore, take some effort to remember that Martin Luther King did not enjoy such widespread approval during his lifetime. His voice was strong and melodious and wonderfully cadenced, but it was, nonetheless, the disturbing voice of dissent. He came to comfort the afflicted, but also to afflict the comfortable. His dissent provoked reaction, as dissent always does. He was called a troublemaker, an agitator, subversive, un-American, a Communist and the most dangerous man in America. He was hated and feared by many and (even worse from his point of view) patronized by those in power.

It has been said that Martin Luther King was a prophet, and I think he was—in the biblical sense of one, who not so much predicts the future, but who sees clearly into the present; who can see what most cannot or will not see. Perhaps the greatest 20th-century novel depicting the pathos and tragedy of Black America is Ralph Ellison's classic, *Invisible Man*. The title is aptly chosen, for it is a theme that runs through the book. The protagonist, a black man says:

> I am invisible, understand, simply because people refuse to see me…When they approach me they see only my surroundings, themselves or figments of their imagination—indeed, everything and anything except me. That invisibility to which I refer occurs because of a peculiar disposition…of their inner eyes, those eyes with which they look through their physical eyes upon reality.

Martin Luther King's vocation was to make visible, to call attention to what most did not want to see: the centuries-old suffering and oppression of his people.

Martin Luther King said that he had a dream. Many of us have heard recordings of his words and felt the stirring power of that speech. The patronizing of Martin Luther King did not, however, end with his death. With him out of the way and not able to object, I am afraid his dream is now more subject to being used and manipulated than ever—interpreted so as to give comfort to the comfortable.

It reminds me of that Coca-Cola ad that ran not so long ago. You may recall the lush meadow filled with people of all races and nationalities holding hands in an immense circle and singing, "I'd like to teach the world to sing in perfect harmony." Often Martin Luther King's dream is seen through the lens of the American dream of middle-class consumer culture, where every place and all people will eventually be converted to one way of life, the American way symbolized by Coca-Cola: sugary sweet, not at all nutritious and ultimately addictive.

Martin Luther King's dream was rooted in his faith, and his faith, Christianity, led him to his stance of nonviolent resistance. He took seriously the Sermon on the Mount: "Blessed are the poor...blessed are the peacemakers...blessed are those who hunger and thirst for justice." He even embraced that seemingly awful and impossible commandment—"Love your enemies." But lest you conclude that as a pacifist he was a fuzzy-headed and sentimental thinker, I invite you to read his essay "My Pilgrimage to Nonviolence." I think you will discover there a subtle and powerful mind at work grappling with the great philosophers and theologians of our times.

He would win the Nobel Prize for Peace and would be praised during his life for his espousal of nonviolence. But even here he was subject to being used and having his message twisted. The '60s saw those long, hot summers where longstanding grievances and pent-up angers would burst out in flames in the ghettos of Watts and Newark and elsewhere. There was much fear in the air of major uprisings and the spread of contagious violence. And Martin Luther King's voice wasn't the only one out there. There were Black Muslims and Black Panthers, people who would say that if you struck them in the face, they would not turn the other cheek; they would hit back, only harder. One can see the appeal Martin Luther King's nonviolence would have for white America.

Few people then or now would really take to heart his philosophy of nonviolence. Mostly nonviolence is seen as a way for those people clamoring for their rights to achieve orderly and peaceful changes; or it is viewed as a smart political tactic for those who would have no hope of achieving victory by means of force. But as a way of life, or a way of ordering social institutions, as a principle to guide a mighty nation–state in its relations with other nations— no, it is not even considered.

There is something a little bit absurd in this national holiday honoring Martin Luther King, the apostle of non-violence, in this country whose government commands a military budget that is greater than the twenty next largest military budgets in the world combined. It is even a bit eerie.

Late in life and against the advice of many of his closest advisors, Martin Luther King began to speak out publicly against the Vietnam War. His first major speech condemning the war was in Riverside Chapel, New York City, on April 4, 1967 (exactly one year before this death), where he would accuse the government in Washington of being "the greatest purveyor of violence in the world today." He would be roundly criticized by the mainstream media, *Time*, the *New York Times*, but also by his own, the leadership of the NAACP. He was told that civil rights and anti-war protest should not be mixed. But he had come to the conclusion that these were but two manifestations of a much larger sickness. It wasn't just about race anymore, for Martin Luther King had begun to make a prophetic judgment upon the economy, speaking about the deep connections linking what he called the "evils" of racism, extreme materialism and economic exploitation, and

74

militarism. A profound change in society would be required. That year he confided to David Halberstam:

> For years I labored under the idea of reforming the existing institutions of the society, a little change here, a little change there. Now I feel quite differently. I think you've got to have a reconstruction of the entire society, a revolution of values.

He was then putting his efforts in the Poor People's Campaign, which was planned to end in a massive demonstration in Washington. But he would interrupt this work to throw his support behind striking garbage workers in Memphis, Tennessee. And, of course, it was there that he met his death.

I can't help but think how much we could use Martin Luther King's strong voice and clear insight in these dark and troubling times. But we are blessed with the memory of his words and the example of his life, and they can still provide guidance and illumination today so many years later. I think, therefore, it appropriate to end by giving Martin Luther King the last word:

> The storm is rising against the privileged minority of the earth, from which there is no shelter in isolation or armament. The storm will not abate until a just distribution of the fruits of the earth enables men and women everywhere to live in dignity and human decency.

AMERICA'S SORROW
AND SHAME

The Moving Wall came to Waltham this past summer. For five days in August this half-scale model of the national Vietnam Veterans Memorial was the centerpiece for solemn ceremonies. Honor guards stood at attention. Bands played patriotic music. Politicians and military officers made speeches. The flag was saluted and pledged to. The clergy gave blessings.

There were also many silent and deeply private moments at the wall. A name would be located and recognized from among the 58,000 inscribed on the black slabs and a flood of memories and emotions would rise up in the reader.

It is proper and just that we remember and honor those who died in the Vietnam War. Each name on the wall represents a unique and precious story of loss and sacrifice. But all those stories are also part of a larger story, the great national tragedy that was the Vietnam War. We do a disservice to those most affected by that war if we are unmindful or untruthful about it. We should not forget the fallen soldiers nor should we forget the war they died in.

Let us then remember that war—no matter how hard and painful that might be.

Let us remember how the government lied about the Gulf of Tonkin incident at the start of the war, and would lie again and again.

Let us remember Vietnam, a small country of rice paddies and villages on which more tonnage of bombs was dropped than in all of World War II.

Let us remember how George W. Bush and most middle-class youth were able to avoid the war; and how the fighting and dying fell on a disproportionate number of Afro-Americans and those from low-income families.

Let us remember the CIA's Operation Phoenix, which was responsible for the extrajudicial executions of thousands of Vietnamese, many of whom were innocent civilians.

Let us remember the search-and-destroy missions which would burn an entire village to the ground in order to "liberate" it.

Let us remember the defoliant, Agent Orange, which poisoned both land and people, causing horrible birth defects among the Vietnamese and a strange illness in American soldiers, which the government would deny for years.

Let us remember that fiendish substance, napalm, and the picture of that girl running in terror and pain as she fled the napalm bombs which had burned the clothes off her body.

Let us remember the My Lai massacre and the photographs of mothers, children and old people lying in lifeless heaps along dirt roads.

Let us remember the "Christmas bombing" when President Nixon ordered B-52's to rain bombs on the heavily populated cities of Hanoi and Haiphong.

Let us remember the undetonated ordinance and landmines which still kill and maim the children of Vietnam.

Let us remember that those politicians and Americans (the so-called silent majority) who most supported the war largely forgot the veterans when the war was over.

Let us remember the over 58,000 Americans and over 1 million Vietnamese who died in that war.

And finally, when we remember that this war did not make us any safer, did not protect our liberties, did not defend us from an aggressor nation or from any real threat to our national security, and that we as a nation seemingly have learned nothing from it, then let us bow our heads in sorrow and shame, and pray that God may forgive America.

U.S. HAS SORDID FOREIGN POLICY HISTORY

With the arrival of the sixth anniversary of the 9/11 attacks, we are likely to hear again the slogan "Never forget 9/11." There is much irony in this simple statement. Not only has 9/11 been forgotten by many Americans, but most don't even know that it happened. I am referring to the first 9/11, that is. The one that occurred in 1973.

This 9/11 was worse than the most recent one. More innocent people were killed, more were terrorized, and an entire country fell under the control of a small band of ruthless men.

This attack did not take place on U.S. soil, but the U.S. was intimately involved. Our government aided and abetted those responsible. As President Bush has made clear, those who assist terrorists are as guilty as those who carry out the deed itself.

On September 11, 1973, General Augusto Pinochet, with the assistance of the CIA, overthrew the democratically elected government of Chile and imposed a military dictatorship. A soccer stadium was converted into a giant prison holding thousands of ordinary people: labor leaders, journalists, clergy, teachers, doctors and community work-ers. Many were summarily executed, many were tortured. Political dissidents who fled the country were hunted down and assassinated under a program called Operation Condor, also with CIA assistance.

The 9/11 coup in Chile was not an isolated or unique event in U.S. foreign policy history. Rather it was more the norm than the exception, not only in Latin America, but throughout the world. For many decades now, U.S. foreign policy has been characterized by similar examples of cynical, brutal and immoral acts.

It is important to bear this is mind as we reflect on the 9/11 anniversary. Given the sordid history of U.S. foreign policy, should we really be surprised that a cynical, brutal and immoral attack would occur on our shores?

Never forget 9/11. Yes, indeed. But we would do well to remember both 9/11's.

WEAPONS YET
TO BE FOUND

Where are all those weapons of mass destruction that the war in Iraq was supposed to be about? You may recall President Bush's State of the Union address in which he declared with great certainty that Saddam Hussein commanded an extensive chemical, biological and nuclear weapons program. He even gave us detailed specifics: 25,000 liters of anthrax, 35,000 liters of *botulinum* toxin, 500 tons of chemical agents, and 30,000 warheads designed to deliver this deadly cargo. Most Americans who supported the war in Iraq did so because they believed the president's words.

Well, it is now over three months since U.S. troops marched into Iraq, and despite intensive efforts to find them, no chemical, biological or nuclear weapons have turned up. And it's not just that they haven't recovered all the alleged quantities of weapons—thousands of liters and hundreds of tons. They haven't found anything at all, not one weapon, not even a thimbleful of lethal material. What then are we to make of this situation so at variance with what we had relentlessly been told for so long? Or, to paraphrase Pete Seeger's famous song, where have all the weapons gone?

I do not believe that the U.S. intelligence services, which are the largest, most powerful, and technologically sophisticated that the world has ever seen, could be so mistaken about what Saddam possessed. I am therefore forced to conclude that there are only two possible answers to the mystery.

One, all those weapons did in fact exist. They cannot be located now, however, because Saddam's vast stockpiles have been cleaned out as thoroughly as the treasures of Baghdad's museum were by international art thieves. Those weapons are now in the hands of terrorists or those who would sell them to terrorists on the underground world market. In this case the war in Iraq must be considered the worst military defeat in U.S. history. The battle for Baghdad was won, but the war was lost, since the stated objective of the war was to prevent weapons of mass destruction from falling into the hands of Al Qaeda or others who would use them against the U.S.

Or two, there never really were all those weapons. If this is the case, then a further conclusion is inescapable: the president and his staff deliberately, intentionally, and with precise calculation, misled the American people.

Either of these two possibilities is, of course, gravely distressing. If I had to judge, however, which of the two posed the greater threat to our freedom and to democracy in our country, I would have to say that it is the one that is also the most likely of the two to be true—that the president lied to us.

U.S. HAS BLOOD
ON ITS HANDS

For decades now, the distinguishing feature of U.S. foreign policy has been its cynicism, immorality and brutality. If you think this is untrue or an exaggeration, please consider the case of Saddam Hussein.

In the months leading up to the Iraq War, we heard much about this man's horrendous deeds. President Bush called him a "psychopathic mass murderer." He was compared to Hitler. He was portrayed as a monster that the world needed to be rid of. He was the very embodiment of evil.

Noticeably absent from the descriptions of Hussein and his deeds, however, was any mention of U.S. foreign policy history and Hussein. In particular, not much was said about U.S. relations with Hussein when he was committing the very worst of his atrocities, the decade of the 1980's.

It was during this decade that Hussein invaded a neighboring country (Iran) without provocation; built up a huge arsenal of chemical and biological weapons; became the first to use chemical weapons on the battlefield since

1925; carried out the bloodiest purges and massacres of political dissidents; committed genocide against the Kurds, using poison gas to kill thousands of men, women and children.

How then did the U.S. react to these monstrous deeds? The record is quite astonishing. Under Reagan and Bush, Sr., the U.S. did the following: removed Iraq from its list of terrorist nations and established normal diplomatic relations with it; blocked a Security Council resolution condemning Iraq for its use of poison gas against Iran; made Iraq into the third largest recipient of U.S. assistance; sent shipments of deadly biological agents to Iraq, including anthrax, botulism and West Nile fever; refused to condemn Iraq, either directly or through the U.N., for its genocide of the Kurds.

President Bush is fond of saying those who assist terrorists share in their guilt. If this standard were applied to those Americans who gave aid and comfort to Hussein, we would have witnessed a startling scene. Sitting in the dock with Hussein and also charged with crimes against humanity would be Ronald Reagan, George Bush, Sr., Dick Cheney, Donald Rumsfeld and Colin Powell.

OSAMA BIN LADEN'S DREAM

A year after 9/11 things were not going well for Osama bin Laden. He was in hiding and on the run. His organization, al Qaeda, which never numbered more than about a thousand, was scattered and in disarray. And worse in his mind, public opinion in Muslim nations and throughout the world overwhelmingly condemned his attacks as crimes and atrocities.

Nevertheless, bin Laden had a dream. In his dream al Qaeda would successfully attack the U.S. a second time. Only this time it would be worse. More Americans would die and many more would be wounded. The attack would also deal a severe blow to the U.S. economy, costing a trillion dollars and plunging it deeper into debt. And most importantly for bin Laden, in his dream, public opinion would turn against the U.S., with many judging the U.S. to be a dangerous and war-like power.

Before he was killed in 2011, bin Laden saw his dream fulfilled. It didn't happen exactly as he had imagined. There would be no one, big attack, but innumerable small ones. And many besides al Qaeda would do the killing. But the end results were the same ones he had desired.

The dream come true for bin Laden was, of course, the Iraq War.

Bin Laden must have been amazed. Less than two years after the worst attack on its own soil, the U.S. was taking its attention away from the perpetrators by launching a full-scale invasion of a country which had absolutely nothing to do with 9/11. Al Qaeda had no presence in Iraq when Saddam Hussein was in power.

During the years that the war raged on in Iraq, bin Laden was comfortably secure in his suburban villa in Pakistan. Al Qaeda crossed into Iraq to join the fighting and to recruit new jihadists. The Taliban steadily won back territory and power it had lost in Afghanistan. And out of the fighting a deadly new weapon was perfected: the improvised explosive device (I.E.D.), which continues to kill Americans to this day.

The Iraq War was a public-relations bonanza for bin Laden. Here was the U.S. invading a Muslim country, half-way across the world, that had not attacked it or threatened to do so. Here was the American president telling the world with great assurance and precise details that Saddam possessed vast arsenals of weapons of mass destruction, and no weapons would ever be found.

And then there were the photographs at Abu Ghraib of Muslim prisoners being tortured and humiliated. Finally, there was the great suffering of the Iraqi people: much of the country in ruins, over 100,000 civilian casualties and 2 million refugees, all making fertile ground for recruitment.

Future historians will no doubt have a hard time understanding the Iraq War. They will wonder how the political establishment of Washington and the majority of Americans could support a war that so readily played into the hands of their chief enemy and made his dream come true. How will they explain that the second attack on America would happen in a distant land and could easily have been avoided?

ETHNIC CLEANSING: IS IT HAPPENING IN THE UNITED STATES?

Joe Porteleki's story at the service two weeks ago startled me. He told us that the night before, as he pondered over how he would relate his experiences in a refugee camp to the Kosovo crisis, an elderly, dignified black man entered his store. With newspaper clippings in hand, Joe revealed to him his thoughts. Yes, the man replied, he too knew something about ethnic hatred; as a boy living in the South, he had witnessed lynchings. Suddenly, what had seemed like a remote, foreign phenomenon was brought home.

It was several hours before it really hit me...actually, I was stunned. Joe's story made me see that right now, right here in our own country, a carefully orchestrated program of ethnic cleansing is taking place! Gone is the mob violence, and in its place is something more sinister, harder to decipher: an official and respectable campaign to cleanse society of black males (and those that look and act like them, those of the underclass). An absurd conclusion? But the figures don't lie, the fantastic figure of 1 million black men in prison (more than all Kosovo refugees?).

And then there is the disturbing fact that all the known elements for ethnic cleansing are in place and operating:

1. The rhetoric of dehumanization
They are animals, vermin, a cancer on society, sub-human, and this is not from the rabble, but from our politicians.

2. The engines of propaganda
News/entertainment media nightly present us with lurid images which inspire hate and fear.

3. The legal/technical apparatus
The prison–industrial complex has grown to enormous proportions. An example: the budget for the drug war in 1993 was $31 billion; the entire welfare budget was $25 billion.

4. The scientific rationale for inferiority
One of the major architects for the war on crime, Professor Charles Murray, an advisor to both Reagan and Kennedy, finally revealed his true thoughts. With his book *The Bell Curve* in 1994, he purported to prove that blacks were genetically inferior! It became an immediate best seller.

The evidence is available. Our criminologists know that there is no correlation between crime rates and incarceration rates. Our sociologists know that crime is a product of socio-economic factors. Why the chilling silence on this issue? Can Germany in the '30s be illuminating for the U.S. in the '90s?

THE PRISON PROBLEM

O ver the course of the last thirty years or so, a radical social experiment has been conducted in our country. What might be the biggest program of social engineering in our nation's history has received widespread support from both Republicans and Democrats, conservatives and liberals.

The intent was to create a safe society cleansed of certain undesirable persons. The result has been to transform the land of the free and home of the brave into the world's greatest incarcerator.

The statistics are staggering. No other country imprisons as many people and at such a rate as the U.S. Of all persons in prison in the world today, 25 percent are in the U.S. That's 2.4 million people, up from about 300,000 in 1970. Out of every 100,000 people living in the United States, 756 are in prison.

Imprisonment rates in other countries don't come close to these figures. The next highest, Russia, is at 629 per 100,000. Most Western European countries are below 100, with the highest, England, at 154. Our neighbor to the north, Canada, is at 139. Even in South America most countries are below 200. Japan has 63.

These comparisons with other countries show how extreme the U.S. experiment in imprisonment has been. Every nation has to deal with the problem of crime in some way. But only the U.S. has adopted prison as its major response and to such an extent. The comparisons show that this need not be the case, that other less severe approaches can work better. Many countries have been much more successful at keeping crime low and we could learn from them.

The U.S. approach is one-dimensional, emphasizing punishment and giving little attention to the causes of crime, the social factors that foster criminal acts. This approach has all the attraction of a simple, big idea: the more people imprisoned and for longer sentences, the less crime there is. More punishment equals less crime. More is better. What's more American than that?

Furthermore, the idea has a self-fulfilling aspect to it. If crime is rising, that's taken as proof that more prisons are needed. If crime is falling, that proves that more punishment works, and more will cause further reductions. Rising or falling crime, either way, more prisons are called for. It's very hard to step out of this mental trap. That's why since 1980 imprisonment rates have continually risen, regardless of fluctuations in crime rates.

But besides being a failed experiment that's enormously costly in human and financial terms, U.S. prison policy has grave political implications. For decades the world's greatest incarcerator was the Soviet Union, something you would expect from a totalitarian society. That the U.S. has replaced the Soviet Union as the world's leading jail keeper should sound the alarm to people who cherish freedom.

Prisons, after all, are places of total control. Every aspect of a prisoner's life is controlled by the government, day and night, every day of the week. As a place of total control, the prison is animated by the spirit of totalitarianism. One could say that each prison, taken as a whole, is a small totalitarian society.

If this fact is acknowledged, a sobering question then becomes unavoidable: How many prisons, how many of these islands of totalitarianism, can a nation sustain without becoming deeply contaminated by them? The spirit of totalitarianism is restless and inventive and does not lie safely contained behind high concrete walls and razor wire.

WALTHAM PEACE VIGIL

Three ago years this upcoming Christmas Eve, with Sue Genser's help, we started the Waltham peace vigil. Since then we have consistently met on the first and third Saturdays of the month from 11:00 a.m. to noon to protest the Iraq War and Occupation. We now meet on the corner of Main Street and Moody Street on both Saturdays.

The first two years of the vigil were well attended with usually 5 to 10 people showing up. This past year, however, two regulars have moved away and few come anymore. Often it's just the two of us. This obviously raised some questions for us: Why don't people come? Why do we still come? Should we continue with the vigil?

We are writing this letter to you and about 25 other friends in Waltham in an effort to answer these questions. We hope to explain why we believe a peace vigil is important and to invite you to join us. But most of all we would like to hear your comments, criticisms, and suggestions regarding what we have written. As we hope to show in this letter, what is most needed in these times, more than anything else, is to think as clearly as possible about the unprecedented situation which faces us. We cannot do that kind of thinking alone. We need each other.

A peace vigil in Waltham

It's important that there be a peace vigil in Waltham.

If there were no peace vigil, there would be no public display in Waltham of dissent to the Iraq War.

If there were no public display of dissent to the Iraq War in Waltham, a strange state of affairs would prevail. Perhaps seventy percent of the people in Waltham would oppose the Iraq War, yet everyone would keep their dissent private, quiet, silent. Not one person would make their dissent public.

This should be a cause of concern...and for careful reflection.

A comparison

With the Vietnam War, the longer the war lasted, the more public dissent there was. With the Iraq War, the longer the war, the less dissent.

With the Vietnam War, it took many years before the government's duplicity and wrongdoing were widely made known. With the Iraq War, the government's duplicity and wrongdoing were widely known quickly. For some, it was obvious even before the war started.

Opposition to the Vietnam War had a deep and profound effect on the country. It took over 18 years before the war-makers could launch another major war, the Gulf War. Opposition to the Iraq War has had little effect. It hasn't even been able to stop the war itself.

Yet, so many reasons for dissent

Has there ever been a time in which there was a clearer and more compelling case for opposing a war? Here is our list of what we think are the most obvious reasons. You may have others to add.

The war is illegal. It violates international law, the U.N. charter, U.S. treaties, etc.

The war is immoral. It violates the just-war theory. It violates our sense of what is right and decent and just.

The war has caused enormous suffering for some Americans and many Iraqis.

The war has set a dangerous new precedent for war, preventive war.

The war is counterproductive to its stated objectives. It has made our country and the Mid-East more unsafe and caused the deaths of more Americans than were killed in the 9/11 attacks.

The war was caused by the duplicity and wrongdoing of the Bush administration and made possible by a fearful and compliant Congress, news media and American public.

Why then no dissent?

With so many strong compelling reasons to oppose the war, the question then must be, Why is there no dissent?

If we cannot answer this question, if we cannot get a good understanding of what we face, we will remain stuck where we are.

Another way of approaching the question is to acknowledge what an amazing achievement we are dealing with.

If the vast majority of a nation's people are against a war, yet the war marches on without interruption, war-makers have truly raised their skill for war-making to a high level, perhaps an unprecedented level.

Let's begin an attempt to answer the question, then, by examining this new way of war-making.

A new era of war-making

While many seemingly have forgotten the lessons of the Vietnam War, some, the war-makers, have learned their lessons well. They have redesigned their product so as to avoid the mistakes that were made in the Vietnam War.

The new improved war the war-makers have designed seems to be based on the following five (5) basic propositions.

1. War is painless

With no draft and a volunteer military, the number of Americans directly involved in war is reduced. Those who are involved face fewer risks as war-making is highly technologized (war by remote control) and only directed against much weaker enemies. Further, the human costs of war are hidden by a compliant news media, and the financial costs are deferred to the next generation.

2. War is love

Careful public relations has raised esteem for the military to a very high level (from the very low esteem following the Vietnam War). All soldiers are heroes now. The key has been to divert attention from what makes a soldier a soldier—the willingness to obey orders and kill other people. Instead, the soldier is portrayed from his non-soldier side as a loving husband, father, neighbor or son (and now mother, wife, etc.). That's what all those yellow ribbons are about. If he is portrayed as a soldier, it's always in the glow of love—love of country, love of freedom, love of his comrades. The enemy, of course, is never portrayed through the eyes of love, but is seen only as one who obeys and kills.

3. War is war on crime

War is no longer a matter of nation fighting nation, or army fighting army. War is a matter of the most powerful military in the world (in history?) fighting certain groups that are deemed to be outlaws, as for example, the Saddam regime or al Qaeda. As a fight against outlaws, that is, criminals, war is now a war on crime (see no. 4 below). Remember Bush's "wanted" posters for al Qaeda or deck of cards for Saddam, et al? Obama has approvingly called the U.S. the "world's reluctant sheriff." War has changed into a form of world-wide policing. Since the police are viewed by many as necessary for keeping the peace, war-as-policing is a form of peace-keeping on a global scale. Therefore, war is peace.

4. War on crime is war

War is based on fear. The more fearful a nation is, the more likely it will go to war. It doesn't matter so much what people fear, as that they be afraid. The objects of fear are easily interchangeable. For about 30 years now Americans have been subject to a carefully designed campaign to raise their fear of crime called the "war on crime." The campaign has been enormously successful. People's fear of crime today is greatly disproportionate to the actual risks of crime. Further, the number of persons in prison in this country grows each year. We have now arrived at the almost unbelievable figure of close to 2.5 million Americans in prison. There are now more people per capita in prison in this country than anywhere else in the world (an incarceration rate unrelated to crime rates, according to criminologists). A people who are so afraid and feel so dependent on protection by the police, on heavily armed men in uniform (and now women), are easily led to wars outside their borders. The domestic war on crime must, by its nature, expand to a global war on crime. Fear and the felt need for protection cannot be contained by borders.

5. *War is normal*

War is no longer a great breakdown or disruption in the normal state of affairs. War is no longer the unusual and temporary. Just as the war on crime is endless, since crime is always occurring, so too is war as a war on crime endless. War has now become what Orwell warned about in *1984*, the normal state of being of the nation. But at the same time that the nation is engaged in ongoing war, for the most part we are barely aware of it. Usually it lurks in the back of our consciousness, like Muzak or white noise, ever present, but we must make an effort to remind ourselves of its presence. This is something not even Orwell had envisioned.

Why dissent has failed

Perhaps then we have an explanation as to why resistance and dissent to the Iraq War has been short-lived and ineffectual. It has failed because it has not yet fully grasped the nature of the new way of war-making that confronts us.

Anti-war protest up to this point appears to have been largely influenced by an understanding of protest that fits the Vietnam War era. It therefore has focused mostly on the wrongdoing and duplicity of Bush et al. and the rationale for the war, much as earlier protest had focused on Nixon et al. and the rationale for that war. But as we hope to have shown, the times today are very different from the days of the Vietnam War. Bush has been greatly discredited and most people are against the war, but while that might have been enough to bring the Vietnam War to an end, it is not enough today.

It appears to us that more is needed than protest against a particular war, that is, a particular application of the new way of war-making. Also, and perhaps even more needed, is protest directed against the new way of war-making itself. For once the premises of the new way of war-making are accepted, war of some kind inevitably ensues, regardless of who is purportedly in charge of the war machinery (first Bush and now Obama), and regardless of public opinion about the war. Protest must challenge these premises.

The vigil as truth telling

The new way of war-making is based on a series of falsehoods. Those promoting the falsehoods are backed up by large amounts of money, large numbers of people, powerful organizations (including both political parties), powerful political friends (including the new president-elect), and wide access to mass media. We, who oppose the new way of war-making, have none of this. But no matter how powerfully promoted the falsehoods are, they are still falsehoods. They are untrue. And the lie is always vulnerable to truth...even if spoken by only one voice.

We believe, therefore, that the basic reason for continuing the vigil is that it is a way to expose the lies of the new way of war-making. By our continued public dissent to the Iraq War, we hope to bear witness to the truth in this way: First, we remind those who see us that the nation remains at war. Secondly, by the simple fact that we oppose this war, even with Bush gone, we affirm the truth that war is not painless, war is not love, war is not the way to peace and war is not normal.

MEMORIES AND THE ETHIC
OF HIROSHIMA

I was born in Los Alamos, New Mexico, the birthplace of the atomic bomb. My father was stationed there during World War II. As a young college graduate with a degree in physics, he was assigned to the Manhattan Project.

Many years later in my living room in Waltham one evening, Mr. Takeshita described to a small group of us what it was like to be in Hiroshima when they detonated the bomb on August 6, 1945.

He told us about a clear blue sky on a summer morning where the sights and sounds of an awakening city spoke of normalcy and routine.

Children marched off to school. Mothers washed breakfast dishes. Old folks sunned themselves on park benches. People from all walks of life filled the streets on their way to work.

And then, without warning, the bomb exploded.

At one point in his story, Mr. Takeshita spoke of stumbling through smoke and ruins and coming upon a young boy who was dying. The boy looked directly at him and pleaded for help. As he spoke, Mr. Takeshita began to softly weep. He then said, "I always cry when I tell of the boy."

I have often wondered about this over the years. Why amidst all that horror did that one boy touch Takeshita so much?

And why after so many years, and telling the story so often, did it still touch him so?

This Monday, August 6, there will be a peace vigil from 7:45 to 8:30 a.m. on the corner of Main and Moody Streets to commemorate Hiroshima. This vigil has been going on for 30 years, since 1982.

I will be going to the vigil. I go in order to affirm a simple, but very basic principle: it is wrong to kill civilians, and it is especially wrong to kill children. It is as wrong in wartime as in peacetime, and it was as wrong in 1945 as it is today.

This principle is at the heart of the ethic of common decency, what is called the natural law. It says that there are some actions which a decent person just will not do, regardless of the consequences.

The atomic bombing of Hiroshima announced to the world, in a bold and dramatic fashion, a very different ethic, one claiming to be more suitable for the technological age into which we had entered.

In this ethic the killing of civilians and children is permissible. Actions formerly thought to be reprehensible were now condoned if they could be shown to achieve a higher goal. This is the ethic that says the ends justify the means.

The ethic of Hiroshima has deeply penetrated American society, becoming a prominent one in both the public and private realm. But beware. The belief that the ends justify the means is a more deadly poison than the radioactive fallout from the mushoom cloud. It can make us into frightful mutants far removed from the kinds of persons we were originally created to be. Renounce and reject it with all your strength.

IV.

ON FAITH

UNEXAMINED BELIEFS

Please forgive me if I add a little heat and pressure to our congregation this morning as we examine the question as to who we are and what brings us together. But if we are to go beyond being merely self-congratulatory, I think we need to look at some obvious reasons as to why we have come to First Parish. We are, after all, very much alike.

An objective observer looking at us from the outside would notice, first of all, what a very homogenous group we are. For the most part, we are white, middle-class, highly educated (and by that I don't necessarily mean erudite, but that we have spent a lot of time in schools), and finally, we are white-collar workers—we don't dirty our hands at the job. I know there are exceptions to this in our church, but they are exceptions. And I know there are other churches similarly homogenous as ours, but of the church denominations, Unitarian–Universalism stands out as being the most white, middle-class, educated and white-collar. I don't know of any black, poor or blue-collar U.U. church.

Now I don't bring this up to make a call for integration

by those different from ourselves. I don't think it's a bad thing that people of similar backgrounds and experiences band together—it's natural. But perhaps it would be wise to do a little thinking on what it means to be a part of the group that we are; and in particular to think on a set of beliefs, which, while largely unexamined, nonetheless play a prominent part in our lives as members of this group. And although they may be called secular beliefs, because they orient life and deal with matters of ultimate significance (that is, truth, evil and suffering and the nature of the good life), I would say that these beliefs are fundamentally religious at heart.

So what then are these beliefs? Three stand out for me.

First, there is the belief in expert knowledge. This belief is based on the idea that we really don't know anything ourselves. For every aspect of life and every moment of life, there is an expert to guide us. Women, for example, have always known how to give birth, breast feed, and raise children. Now they need experts to tell them how. People always knew how to grieve—now they go to experts on grieving. This dependency on experts has eroded other forms of knowledge: tradition, personal experience, community mores, the advice of neighbors or family. At one time people believed in the authority of the Pope on matters of faith. Today many believe in the authority of innumerable popes on innumerable subject matters.

Second, is the belief in safety—which we might call an obsession. We hear this word so much. We hear of safe schools, safe streets, playgrounds safe of bullies, our groups must be safe and supportive. There is that oxymoron, safe sex. Swing sets are no longer safe (as we learned from our day care). We see three-year-olds on tricycles made safe by helmets. At Waltham Family Safety Day, children had their fingerprints and dental impressions taken—for safety's sake. The dream here is one of creating a new Garden of Eden, where bad things do not happen to good people. The reality is a nightmare of fear and suspicion, of growing dependence on government and police protection, of more people per capita in prison than anywhere else on earth.

Finally, there is the belief in competitive achievement. Achievement in the classroom, the athletic field or concert hall is highly prized and serves as a prelude to achievement in the marketplace of careers. The achiever stands out as a winner surrounded by the many losers. The achiever is driven partially by a fear of falling from grace into the world of losers, but also by a sense that achievement is a mark of one's own virtue, of one's goodness. The converse of this is that losers get what they deserve, they are unworthy. This belief is very convenient in a society where those in the bottom third income bracket are more and more considered to be losers.

You have probably concluded that the three beliefs I have been describing are not unique to Unitarian–Universalism. I would say that these beliefs are now part of the religious cosmology of most white, middle-class Americans, including members of Christian churches and Jewish synagogues, replacing in importance, for example, original sin or the mystery of the Incarnation. Wouldn't it be ironic then, if in a non-creedal church such as First Parish, these beliefs were first brought to light and subject to critical reflection and discussion?

SOME THOUGHTS
ON WORSHIP

I take it as some kind of sociological fact that we are by nature religious, worshipping creatures. It seems that, whether we call ourselves religious or not, we must worship something, have faith in something. This in and of itself is neither good nor bad. The essential question is, what is being worshipped?

Certainly we can think of examples of religious practices, of worship, which we would not want anything to do with, which are even abhorrent to us. Worship sometimes calls for blood, and as the historical record shows, lots of it at times. And we know how any religion can be *used* by people; either as an escape from their fears, insecurities and sufferings (religion as a warm fuzzy blanket or narcotic) or as a way of getting divine beings to get one what he wants (worship as superstition—"say the right words, do the right ritual and you'll get the desired result"). We also know how religion is used to justify oneself, one's actions or politics. "God is on my side" is a kind of bludgeon, handy in an argument with one's wife or political adversary.

Now I think that the old Jewish prophets were condemning just this kind of use of religion when they spoke of the worship of idols. They understood idols to be the work of human hands, empty vessels representing nothing more than the projection of their makers, the real object of worship of idols being the self. That is why idols are ultimately about power, power over others, power over nature; they spring from self-worship, egocentricity.

Unfortunately I think we all have a tendency to idolatrous self-worship—no matter what our faith is. My faith, Christianity, bears witness to this. Church history is a long tale of lapses into the idolatry of power, institutional or individual power, which is a perversion of its expressed faith—that worship centers on love—the unfathomable mystery of the Incarnation, that God became man and suffered and died for our sins as the supreme act of love.

I wish to make a second point while we are reflecting on the meaning of worship. Religion to be religion does not necessarily require a belief in a specific divine being, a god, nor does it need a theology—it does need worship, however.

Presently as we stand at the end of this century, this millennium, I think we are witnessing the triumph of a new world religion, one that is not recognized as a religion because it does not call itself one, or have the usual religious associations, a god or theology. The origins of this religion, however, can be pinpointed with accuracy. It arose in Western Europe, first emerging in the Christian churches, and then coming into full development free of any necessary connections with them, becoming in the process more powerful, more catholic, that is, universal, and more dominant that any church before it.

The gospel of this new religion, the good news, is that man has conquered nature—and human nature—and, given enough time and money, the victory shall be complete. Total domination shall be ours—if we have faith. We have witnessed the splitting of the atom and the splicing of genes; the old mysteries and gods have been banished. Nature is now mere stuff to be used, torn apart, recombined, made into something new, a new creation. Finally we can be as gods, we can create the world. A new Eden awaits us all, a manmade paradise, but only if we have faith. There are those who lack this faith. However, we don't call them heathens any longer. Rather they are "uneducated" or, better yet, "underdeveloped."

In any event it is just a matter of time before they become developed, become truly human, converted, that is. They have no choice, you see; this religion is the only way, the only truth—you can't stop progress.

But what is being worshipped here? Isn't it power, plain and simple, that is being worshipped in this new religion? And perhaps an ancient warning should ring in our ears.

The prophets said that idols had eyes but could not see, and ears but could not hear, and that those who made them soon became like them. (What we worship we become.)

Have you noticed how people speak today. They no longer speak, they "communicate." They don't listen, they access "information." Both ideas and grief are "processed." People ask for "feedback." Gazing into the other's face has become "interface." And of course minds are now "hardwired."

A deep and radical change in self-perception is indicated here. Perhaps this is our most severe ecological disaster, one of the spirit; the diminishment of our capacity for authentic worship, a loss of soul.

WHAT I BELIEVE
IS SIMPLE...

What I believe is simple...sort of. I believe what Jesus taught us so many years ago, that it all really comes down to just two things, loving God and loving our neighbor. Simple...but also hard. Hard to put into practice. Hard even to understand at times. It was the lawyer after all who asked Jesus, Who then is my neighbor?

In 1993 Sue and I and our two sons took a trip to Mexico to visit an old friend. Twenty years before I had attended a Spanish language school my friend had founded in Cuernavaca. Speaking on the phone before the trip, my friend told me that Cuernavaca had gone from a population of 90,000, when I was there, to over one million. I was startled. It was hard to imagine such an explosive growth in size.

After we arrived and stayed awhile in Cuernavaca, I saw what I had expected: large, sprawling settlements on the edge of the city composed of makeshift shelters built from industrial refuse—plywood, tin, plastic, even cardboard— places we would call slums or shanty towns. Yet, there was something I was expecting which I didn't see, and this surprised me. I didn't see what you will find in any major city in the U.S.—bands of homeless people living on the streets.

Over dinner one day with my friend I asked him about this. Was my observation true? If so, how could this be? Although my friend was not a native to Mexico, he was a person of immense learning and an acute observer of Mexican life. He replied that, yes, it was true and then explained that in Mexico, no matter how poor a person may be, he or she still felt capable of offering hospitality to another, even if it is only a little space in the corner of one's shack.

Over the years I have often thought of my friend's words. Hospitality is, of course, one form of love of neighbor. The Samaritan extended it to the beaten-up Jew lying in a ditch. Some people practice it better than others. I saw a poor society where it was practiced well. By contrast, in our society, a rich society, homelessness is a persistent problem. Perhaps for us as Christians, the existence of the homeless, and even of homeless shelters, is a great judgement on the kind of society in which we live.

You may have heard of an incident that occurred in Hartford, Connecticut, last year. It was caught on surveillance cameras and widely reported in the news media. An older man was crossing a downtown street at rush hour when he was hit by an suv, which then fled. The man lay on the street injured while traffic drove around him. People on sidewalks kept walking. Some stopped and looked. Nobody, however, not one, went over to the injured man. It wasn't that all were unconcerned. Many called 911. One man's call was recorded. "Please hurry," he pleaded. "The man seems really hurt." Yet, somehow, it never occurred to him to go himself over to the man. How was this all possible, two thousand years after Jesus told the Good Samaritan parable?

The Samaritan was touched by the plight of the Jew and felt called to make a personal response. We in our rich society face barriers to that touch and to that call. The barriers are the result of institutionalization. For every suffering person there is, at least on paper, an institution or agency with trained personnel who are paid to attend to that person. It's their job. The personal response is replaced by an impersonal, institutional response, and as our institutions grow strong, our capacity for hospitality grows weak. Ultimately we are confronted with a temptation the Samaritan did not know: the enticement to be free of the great challenge of living in accordance with the Gospel.

A STRANGE STORY

A strange story this is about wise men coming from the east. Magi they were called. A word which conjures up our words *magic* and *magician*. They studied the night sky, the stars and planets, and came from the land of the great empires of Babylon and Persia, where startling discoveries were made in astronomy and mathematics. Behind the veil of nature, the Magi saw patterns and laws which set them apart from other men and made them useful to those in power. Unlike the common people who saw the world as a playground for hordes of gods, who like humans were capricious and unpredictable, the Magi's cosmos was based on ideas and abstractions; not Venus but love, not Mars but war. They pondered the All, the One, and marveled at the impersonal order of the universe. As an elite possessed of esoteric knowledge, of nature's mysteries and secrets, they were esteemed by the powerful and rewarded with the comforts of that world. Their connection with political power is seen today in the popular tradition of calling them the "Three Kings."

And then they saw the star and something was set

ablaze in their hearts. Without quite understanding why, they knew they had to make that journey. Not an easy thing in those days. "The ways deep, the weather sharp, the very dead of winter," writes T. S. Elliot in his poem of the Magi. And there was the threat of brigands, the vast desert to cross and the expense of such a caravan. Yet they went, and after a while the Magi entered the land of the Jews. The Jews, those odd people, who claimed that their King David was also a wise man, he who wrote the psalms and once sang, "like a deer that longs for the water brook, my soul longs for you oh Lord."

In Jerusalem, the Magi ask, "Where is the baby born to be the king of the Jews?" We read that Herod and all Jerusalem became very troubled. We know why Herod was upset, but why were the Jews? Could this be the one? they no doubt wondered. The Jews had been waiting for so long, expectant for so long. They knew they had a special place in human history. They had been especially chosen and one day they, as a nation, would shine out like a beacon for all the other nations. For they had been drawn near to One whose very name was too holy to pronounce; One so different from the other, lesser gods.

The Jews understood this One as having created the universe. Not part of or in the world, their God held the entire world in His hands and sustained it with His breath. The Jews would not attempt to conceptualize their God or fashion images of Him. He could not be seen. Moses had only seen the hem of His robe. Uniquely transcendent and remote, this God was also inexplicably personal, speaking through the mouths of the prophets, urging compassion for widows and the dispossessed, condemning the hardness of heart and idolatry of the people, and holding them to an exacting moral code. Through their relationship with this God, the Jews came to believe they had a unique destiny. There was a special purpose and meaning to life, since human history was set on a path that broke free from the endless cycle of nature of the pagan world, the dreary round of endless repetition, where nothing new was under the sun. A glorious, but mysterious future was coming. But when? Poor Israel, for only a few years under David and Solomon had she known prominence. But mostly as a nation Israel was a pawn of a succession of great powers: Egypt, Assyria, Babylon, Greece and now the Romans. However, a leader had been promised to the Jews, a Messiah, God's holy anointed who would bring Israel to its glory and free her from captivity. Yes, the arrival of the Magi troubled the Jews. They so longed for a mighty king.

The Magi leave Jerusalem, and here the story gets even stranger. We hear of their joy when they see the star again, and, guided to the child, they kneel down and worship him, giving him gifts fit for a king. But what kind of king was this? No palace here, but a shelter for farm animals. Instead of perfumes and incense, the smell of sheep and goats. And for a cradle, no silks or cushions, only rough wood and straw. This royal family far from home and unwelcome, would soon be fugitives fleeing for their lives under cover of darkness. The lowliest of lowly, the most unkingly of kings.

How, then, were the wise men to understand this? They, who had relied on the superior powers of their intellect, which had been so good to them, giving them honors and privilege, and which now was of no use here, they had to open themselves to another source of knowledge, a new capacity for knowing, which to those outside looked like the utmost foolishness. Risking everything, their wealth, prestige and very lives, they put their trust in the child and defied cruel Herod, whose fury would know no limits, who would spill the blood of the many innocents.

The Magi escaped, however, and returned home to their lands. And while we learn no more about them, the story, of course, does not end there. We will hear about the child, how he grew in power and wisdom, how his people wanted him to be king, proclaiming him to be the Messiah, leading him triumphantly into Jerusalem on a donkey, how he was betrayed by the leaders of his nation and executed by the Romans with a sign above his cross which read "King of the Jews." Again, not much of a king, this king whom the Magi once worshipped.

But here is where the story becomes most truly strange. Wise and holy men and women, heirs of the Magi, began to appear in increasing numbers in the ancient world, speaking of the child, proclaiming that he was the Messiah, and more, that he was God's Son and that the Holy One of Israel, the Absolute, the Perfect, the Eternal, the most transcendent of gods, had become the most tangible, had become incarnate, touchable, had taken on flesh and blood and lived closely and intimately with a small group of friends, and that He is present at any place and moment when one who is thirsty is given a drink. And most astonishingly, these men and women were convinced that their vocation in life was to seek His face in that other who stood in front of them within the reach of their loving arms.

What a strange, wondrous, frightful, incomprehensibly sweet story—the Epiphany of Matthew's Gospel.

MY FAITH

My faith is that of a Christian, which as I understand it centers around two main articles of faith. First, that God is the creator of the heavens and earth, of all that is seen and unseen. And secondly, that at a particular moment in history, God became incarnate, became a man and walked on this earth, in the flesh, just as much as you and I do.

Not long ago I was given an insight into my faith by a person who described herself as an atheist. We had met at a dinner party and somehow the conversation had turned to religious upbringing and belief. She had grown up in Unitarian churches and for most of her life had been a deeply convinced atheist. At some point in the discussion she announced in a slightly argumentative fashion that just as she had stopped believing in Santa Claus at a certain time in her life, so as she grew older she stopped believing in God. I made no response but quickly tried to turn the conversation to other topics.

Later, though, I thought about this statement. I imagined the woman as a young girl looking at the Christmas tree after her discovery. She now knew that there was no Santa Claus, but then there still were all those presents in their bright colored paper. If Santa Claus did not bring them, someone else must have.

In the Christian tradition, all that is, the natural world, all the people we know, everything, has something of the quality of a gift. And every gift to be a gift must come from a giver who through the gift expresses intent, will and love. God in the Christian view, as Creator, is the All-Giver who expresses His unbounded love through the universe.

It is said that God has written two books for us by which we may come to know Him: the book of Nature and the book of Scripture.

Scripture, the Bible, is really a collection of many books, over sixty some, written by a host of largely unknown authors, over a span of centuries, in a variety of literary genres, telling the most unusual stories about the most motley of characters: kings and queens, yes, but also slaves and barren women, wandering nomads, madmen, prophets and prisoners. Through it all, we learn of the conviction that God is present and active in the lives of these people, in the unique circumstances that surround each one of them, whether grand or mundane.

And what we see is that the God of Abraham, Isaac and Jacob and, later, of Mark, Matthew, Luke and John, is principally concerned with how people live. Time and again, people are condemned for their hardness of heart. This is not your conventional morality, for what makes hardness of heart so unsettling is that it causes a blindness such that one cannot see one's own faults. We are all susceptible to it, and there are certain telltale signs of its presences: complacency; self-satisfaction; the love of comfort, prestige or power. There is no security either to be found in human moral institutions. Rome and Jerusalem were the most sophisticated political and religious authorities of their time, and they condemned Jesus to death.

What emerges in Scripture, coming into brilliant focus in the passion of Jesus, is a certain way of life, which is something quite different from mere adherence to moral codes or rules. Remember, it was the despised and looked-down-upon of Jesus's time who were most open to His words and the way of life He describes. After all these centuries, His words still speak to us today:

> Look at the birds of the air, they do not sow or reap or store away in barns, and yet your heavenly Father feeds them.
>
> Are you not much more valuable than they?
>
> A grain of wheat remains a solitary grain unless it falls into the ground and dies but if it dies it bears a rich harvest.

FRANZ JÄGERSTÄTTER

A PROPHET FOR OUR TIME

One night in 1938, in the Austrian village of St. Radegund, a young farmer had a dream. The farmer, Franz Jägerstätter, dreamt of a magnificent new train with a powerful locomotive and gleaming carriages. People from everywhere flocked to the train which overflowed with passengers. While gazing at the wonderful sight, Franz heard a mysterious voice tell him the train's destination: it was going to hell. He then frantically tried to convince everyone to abandon the train, but no one listened and the train continued on its journey.

At first Franz was puzzled by his dream but at some point he came to understand its message. The train symbolized National Socialism, the ideology that had swept Hitler into power and whose rule Austria had overwhelmingly voted to accept. The dream showed National Socialism to be diabolical, a power that would bring physical and spiritual ruin to the country.

Franz was a devout Christian, the sexton in his local Catholic church. He had not always been that way though. As a youth he had the reputation of being somewhat wild, getting into gang fights and fathering a child out of wedlock. But he would meet and then marry Franziska, who brought maturity and spiritual depth into his life.

When war came, Franz was eventually drafted into the military. At the time, he had a family of three young girls, the eldest not yet six years old. He faced a hard decision. He knew that Hitler's war was unjust and he knew the evil that the Nazis represented. But he also knew that resistance meant certain death. Nevertheless, Franz decided he could not betray his faith. He refused to become a soldier.

Most people in his village were upset with Franz. Many tried to convince him to change his mind, even Franziska at first. His parish priest and later his bishop would counsel him to cooperate. They spoke to him about his responsibility for his daughters, about obedience to authority and the evil of communist, atheist Russia. But Franz was resolute. He would not budge. On August 9, 1943, Franz was beheaded. He was 36. After the war, when his village put up a commemorative plaque listing its men killed in the war, Franz's name was left out. Some even shunned Franziska.

In 1961, Franziska was interviewed by an American professor, Gordon Zahn. Somehow Gordon had heard the story of Franz while doing research into the two questions that haunted his adult life. Why had a predominantly Christian country, Germany, capitulated to Hitler? And, secondly, why were the two worst wars in history, World War I and World War II, fought by Christian nations, Christians killing Christians? Gordon would write a book about Franz, *In Solitary Witness*, which would bring his little-known story out to the wider Church community.

And then in 2007 an amazing thing happened. With the approval of Pope Benedict XVI, a German, Franz was beatified, a step which will lead to his being officially declared a saint.

Franz was a prophet. Rooted in faith, he declared a truth people did not want to hear. He also shared the fate of many of the prophets. He was killed by those he was trying to save. And while he spoke to his own countrymen and women, in their time and place, just like the prophets of old, he continues to speak to us today, across time and place. What is Franz saying to us now, in Waltham, at Christ Church?

BUSH, BIN LADEN SHARE

One of the strangest things about this so-called war against terrorism is the language President Bush uses to defend it—in many ways his rhetoric matches that of Osama bin Laden. Four similarities in particular stand out for me.

First, both men tell us that this is a great war of good vs. evil. Each believes that his side represents pure good and the other pure evil. Since the enemy is portrayed as the very embodiment of evil in this absolutist way of thinking, presumably one is free in good conscience to make him into an object of hate; a non-person, that is, a thing fit only for extermination.

Secondly, both men, in their own way and seemingly unaware of the profanity of their words, call this war a "holy" war. To one it's a Jihad and the other a Crusade.

Thirdly, both men use people's outrage at the killing of innocent civilians as a way to justify their commitment to the use of violence. Bush asks Americans to remember the 3,000 men and women killed in New York City and Washington, D.C.; bin Laden tells the Arab world not to forget the 500,000 children who have died in Iraq as a result of U.S. sanctions and bombing, or the Palestinian teenagers gunned down by U.S.-supported Israeli soldiers.

Finally, and not surprisingly, both men claim that God is on their side. Once again God is called upon to sanction the violence men do to each other.

But I wonder…at whose feet do these men really worship? I know they claim to be Christian and Muslim, adherents of two faiths that have a common tradition and common belief in the One the prophets of Israel knew as Jehovah. Yet, I suspect that in their hearts Bush and bin Laden have faith in another god, who demands human sacrifice and whose thirst for blood is never slaked. The ancient Romans also knew this god well but they called him by name—Mars, the god of war.

THE GREATEST
FORCE FOR GOOD

I was startled to hear President Bush, a professed Christian, make a blatantly un-Christian, even heretical, statement at the Republican National Convention. In his acceptance speech, he declared that our country is "the greatest force for good on this earth." Our faith tells us differently, of course. The greatest force for good on earth, as it is in heaven, is God's loving presence and activity in our lives. And it is the Church (the Bride of Christ), not the Nation or the State, that is God's means for the greatest good possible, the salvation of men and women everywhere.

President Bush's error is not a trivial matter, nor is it unique to him or his political party. It is as old as the Bible, which warns us against the temptation of giving ultimate significance to ourselves or our works. The prophets called this idolatry, the worship of the products of our own hands. Graven images can be idols, but so too can a nation's institutions, achievements, political system or way of life. Given the amount of power concentrated in his hands, President Bush's exhortation to idolatry warrants our strongest public admonishment.

WHERE FAITH
AND DUTY COLLIDE

The repeal of the "don't ask, don't tell" rule has ended the military's presumption that gays do not make good soldiers. I don't know enough about the issue to form an opinion as to whether this is true or not of gays. I do believe, however, that there is a particular group of people for whom this presumption is true, at least potentially. I am referring to those of the Roman Catholic faith.

I do not say this out of any religious prejudice. I myself am Catholic. I have come to this conclusion solely by examining Catholic doctrine and history.

The Church teaches that a person's first and ultimate loyalty is not to the State (the government, the president, the military, etc.). It is owed to God. For Catholic soldiers this means that the Commander-in-Chief and all other commanders do not have absolute authority over them. According to their faith, they should not obey orders which conflict with their primary allegiance. There may be times when being a good Catholic demands that one be a bad soldier.

One such time occurred in the life of Franz Jägerstätter. He was a devout Catholic who refused to fight in the

German army in World War II because he knew Hitler was waging an unjust war. He was executed in 1943. The Catholic Church beatified him in 2007, a process which will lead to his being declared an official saint. For Catholics, saints are models of Christ-like behavior, persons to be emulated. As we know, however, most German Catholics did not follow Jägerstätter's example. Tragically, they acted as good soldiers instead of good Catholics.

More recently, Catholic soldiers in America were faced with a similar choice. In 2003, Pope John Paul II and the American bishops spoke out clearly and unequivocally against the proposed, pre-emptive war against Iraq. At that moment a great opportunity was presented to Catholic soldiers. Had enough of them refused to fight that war because it was unjust, the invasion of Iraq might not have been politically or militarily feasible. Catholic soldiers would have faced imprisonment and other harsh consequences, but think of the good that would have come of this. So many thousands of U.S. soldiers would not have been killed, crippled or disfigured. So many hundreds of thousands of Iraqis would not have shared a similar fate.

But this of course did not happen. Catholic soldiers acted as good soldiers. Catholic doctrine, however, does not change and there remains the example of the saints. We can still hope and pray that some day Catholic soldiers will refuse to fight in an unjust war, and when that day comes the military might want to adopt a "don't ask, don't tell" policy for Catholics. What a great and glorious day that would be for the Catholic Church.

V.

A SENSE OF PLACE

THE BODY, PLACE,
AND SPACE

What do we mean by this simple phrase, "a sense of place?" And how does one have a sense of place? Well, to have a sense of place, we need, first of all, places —that's obvious enough, and, secondly, we need places that can be grasped by the senses, all of the senses. Do we have such places, not just theoretically, but in our own lives?

I find in my life that instead of places, I am surrounded by space. Space is place rationalized, standardized and homogenized. It is as if the marvelously diverse and precious places around us have been put into a techno-economic blender. Push the right button and out comes the right space; highway space, shopping-mall space, hospital space, cubicle space, suburban space, penitentiary space. Space is place colonized. Whether the scene is Boston, London or Tokyo, places are everywhere looking the same. Do you know where you are inside a Hilton Hotel, an airport or a multi-lane highway? You could be anywhere...or nowhere.

Space is primarily a concept, a mental construct imposed on nature and society. Being mind-dominated, space disconnects us bodily from where we are and who we are with. The primary sense used in space is sight. And sight is the one sense that most permits detachment. Remote and uninvolved, we can see in space, but not touch or smell or taste—we have little experience of being bodily present. Our experience in space is not much different from watching images on a screen. Can this help to explain why watching images on a screen is so popular today?

In contrast to space, place is tangible. It literally touches us on many levels. When we look at the stars on a winter night, the cold is part of the seeing. When we walk in the woods, there is a certain strain on the legs. Sitting in a room with friends, we feel the atmosphere of mutual joy right in the gut. Places engage us fully; we take them in as we breathe. Our presence is an embodied presence, a sensed presence. And only when we are so engaged bodily can the mysterious uniqueness of each place and each person be apprehended. So in this sense, we might say that it is the body that makes a place.

THOUGHTS ON THE VIDEO
NO PLACE TO HIDE

What stood out most for me from watching the video was the image of the woman whose father had been killed. We see her amidst the rubble of what had once been his home. She is in the throes of grief, weeping and at times waving her arms. She tells us how mutilated her father's body was by the bombs. Her presence at that moment seems so strong that the magic of the video takes place—I felt she was talking directly to me and I was there with her surrounded by the piles of brick.

But I wasn't there of course; the camera was. If I was there, my experience would have been so much different. If in our real lives we are confronted with a scene of tragedy similar to this one, how would it be, what would we do? Perhaps approach the gathered crowd and ask what had happened, maybe speak with a friend or relative. But march right up to the grief-stricken, a total stranger? No. We would be tentative, respectful, gently inquiring if there was something to be done to help. But the camera doesn't have to act so. It has a certain license, an imperial license; it demands that it be spoken to.

We never learn the woman's name or that of her father. In fact we don't learn anything about this woman, how she grasps that most essential moment, how she suffers it, what meaning she can find in it and how she weaves it into the fabric of *her* life. Instead, the moment is seized by the camera. Quite literally seized, materialized into video tape, to be handled and manipulated by technicians, cut up and spliced, and edited to fit into what the producer has decided to be the film's "message," *his* message.

It's extraordinary, really. A most private moment, one saturated with personal intimacy, is diminished of anything but the barest of elements and then displayed before innumerable strangers in a distant land. But only for a few seconds! Yes, it is only shown for less than half a minute and we are on to the next scene. An incredible, strange kind of violation of this woman has taken place.

Am I being overly imaginative here, pushing a rarified sensibility too far? But look how viewing this scene affects us. One could not help but be moved by it, it was so poignant. Yes, it was as if this woman was speaking directly to us, one to one. Watching her, I felt a sweep of emotions: from sorrow, pity and anger to dread and fascination—"Ah, so that's what it's like. I wonder how I would take it."

But the emotions go nowhere. In the back of my mind I know it's only a video; I will never meet this woman, this scene will quickly pass, it makes no demand on me. The experience is so essentially different from being face to face with a person, right here, right now, which always presents a question, a challenge: how do I respond, what do I say or not say, what do I do or not do to this person in front of me?

Ultimately, the video experience is a fraudulent one. It gives the semblance of a personal relationship, even with emotional attachment, yet there is no substance to it. It is all shadows. No opportunity to take in who this person is, to respond to this particular person at this particular time and place. As a psuedo-experience, an illusionary one, perhaps the video marks the diminishment of our very capacity for experiencing, that is, of our capacity for being human.

THE CAUCASIAN ROCK
IN THE YEAR 2003

There is much wisdom in this old myth about Prometheus and the gift of fire. Like the Garden of Eden story, it is a foundational myth, telling us something about our origins, what our place is in the world, and what our relationship is to nature and to the gods, to the supernatural.

According to the ancient Greeks, it's the use of fire that distinguishes us from all the other creatures. Prometheus's brother, Epimetheus (whose name means "afterthought"), had the task of distributing an assortment of gifts to the living beings on earth. To some he gave great strength and to others swiftness, some received thick fur or hard scales, some were given the ability to fly or swim. When it came to mankind, however, he had handed out all that he had been entrusted to give, leaving men and women vulnerable and weak compared to the other creatures. So it was up to Prometheus (whose name means "forethought") to steal fire from the gods for us. And what a gift it was, providing warmth in cold weather, light at nighttime, protection from even the most ferocious of beasts. With it, tools could be forged from metals, clay baked and food cooked. Men and women became the tool-using creatures; the cultivators of plants, domesticators of animals, the builders of cities and the makers of cultures.

There is, however, a warning in this myth, a sense that certain limits and boundaries exist, which should not be crossed. Looming in the background is the possibility of the revenge of the gods for acts of unrestrained pride or hubris. Prometheus pays the price on the Caucasian rock—a reminder to us of the perils of exceeding our nature, of venturing where we don't belong, of transgressing the order of things.

The myths of the Greeks are far from us today. To modern ears they seem strange and foreign, at most quaint, colorful tales with little to tell us about our present condition unless it's to confirm for us our superiority over our more primitive and unenlightened ancestors. In much the same way the creation myth of Genesis has also been cast aside as out of date.

But this is not to say that we don't have our own myths in the present age of science and technology. People of every society must have a collective sense of themselves, of who they are, of how they fit into the scheme of things—a foundational myth. Ours is also bound up with fire like the Prometheus tale, but I think that our myth is unprecedented, unlike anything any other people, in any other culture, in any other time, have ever believed.

Fitting for the uniqueness of the myth is the means by which it is conveyed; a totally new medium is employed. We have left behind the world of orality, and the world of literacy also, the oral songs of Homer and the literate compositions of Aeschylus. We have even abandoned the plastic arts those worlds made possible. What we have now to tell our modern myth (or should I say feverish dreams?) is something only recently manufactured: the spectral image.

The particular image that I am speaking of as projecting our foundational myth is so commonplace today that it has become trivial, appearing on coffee mugs and T-shirts, on posters and in advertisements. It doesn't purport to be a myth-generating image, only a depiction of what is, of simple reality, and therein lies its mesmerizing power.

I ask you to bear with me as we examine this seemingly benign picture, for I believe it to be most toxic at bottom, rooting in our hearts and imaginations an image of ourselves and nature that chains us to our own kind of Caucasian rock of endless frustration, pain and anxiety.

The image I am speaking of is the photograph of the earth from space, of the blue globe suspended in black emptiness.

The first thing to notice about this photo is how unique it really is as an object of sight; what I would refer to as its extraordinary epistemological status. You and I have never seen this object, the earth, and only a tiny few of the people who have ever lived have ever really seen it with their own eyes. Yet we tend to think of this object as we do with any other we have seen, like a tree, a rock or a person's face; things we have the capacity to see in our everyday life. In our minds, however, we don't make a distinction between the blue globe and those objects that we can truly see. And thus, from the start, we are deceived by the blue globe as to the unnaturalness of what we are being shown.

The blue globe also hides from us its history and the questionable means by which it is made, beguiling us into a suspension of thought concerning past and present, and cause and effect. Some effort of the memory is needed to recall that this photo has become a historical possibility only through the development of the most deadly weapons, the most lethal killing instruments, ever invented. This harmless-looking photo is a child of the military–industrial complex. And with such parentage violence is inherent to its nature. Think of any blast-off, think of all that explosive fire that is needed to propel the camera-carrying rocket through the earth's atmosphere; a fiery violence far beyond Prometheus's gift.

So much fire, so much violence to make this image. And why? Because the earth resists it and pulls all objects to her in a tight embrace. To sever these earthly bonds, to break the natural connectedness, only great violence can do that.

The photo doesn't indicate any of this, though; it comes to us after the fact, so to speak. But if we look carefully we can see the disconnectedness, the broken bonds, can't we? There is something haunting about this image. Has there ever been a more alienated view imaginable, alienated from the earth? As we look, we are apart, distant, remote from our home the earth, where from any point on which we stand we are offered an incredible variety of forms, shapes, colors, views, and vistas—all of this is reduced to a disc, featureless and unrecognizable, about the size of a tennis ball and about as interesting.

When we look at this photo, think for a moment about the perspective we are made to assume.

To whom is this way of seeing appropriate, seeing the earth from a point so far away from it, the earth appearing so small and fragile, something that could be held in one's hands? It is, of course, the view of God, or the gods, the view from the heavens, a position even higher than Mount Olympus. And perhaps this is the secret spell of the blue globe photo, its myth-generating power. No longer a creature of the earth, we have become more than even Prometheus; we have become gods—or so it whispers to us.

It is so seductive—really, for we have acquired in fact god-like powers. We can now destroy the blue globe by turning it into a ball of fire with our nuclear flames. Or perhaps more slowly, we will destroy the natural world with our poisons or many technological fires which might warm the atmosphere beyond its suitability for creatures.

But our doleful powers don't end with only that kind of destruction, for we have now moved from the Manhattan Project to the Genome Project. We have it within our capability to engineer new life forms; we can manufacture living creatures just as we do our automobiles or laptops, or any other mass-produced commodity. Where once people strove to live in harmony with nature, achieving a certain balance with her powers, as the tale of

Prometheus suggests, we now conquer and subdue nature and even remake her into one of our many artifacts. We have converted the natural world, in our minds and our projects, into mere raw material for our production processes; which can refashion all that exists, both human and natural, according to our own designs and plans. We have thus arrived at the Final Solution to the problem of nature.

And finally when we contemplate our new powers and the unfathomable dangers that they impose, we deem ourselves capable of the ultimate of god-like abilities; for now we must "save the earth." So there you have it—Destroyer, Creator and Savior—all the powers of the gods are ours whether we like it or not. Isn't this the siren song of the blue globe photo?

But the Greek and Jewish stories are there to remind us, even today, that we were not meant to be gods, that we have a place on earth that is unique and fitting for us, upon which we can stand on our own two legs, and it is good and enough; and can be enjoyed even with that very simple but most human act of resting our eyes on a natural wonder that lies within our view; like a tree, a rock or a person's face.

MUSIC AND THE
DISINCARNATION
OF THE WORD

We live in a society that has lost its song. This is not unique to our society. It is a world-wide phenomenon. The more advanced the society, the higher its so-called standard of living, the less song there is in its culture. If you doubt that this is true, just ask the people around you (at least those who don't go to church) when it was that they last sang a song with others.

Music means something fundamentally different for us today than it did for our ancestors. For them, music was what occurred in their presence; either they themselves made it, or others whom they personally knew sang or played the instruments. This kind of music was essential to community life. It helped give the "I" the experience of being a tangible "we." In that sense, music was like speech, that mysterious activity that distinguishes us from all other of God's creatures and that has the power to bind us together in an intimate conversation. Song, of course, is one form of speech.

All that has changed with the advent of telecommunication, with the arrival of electricity and the loudspeaker. Today most of the music that people hear comes out of a box of some sort. The boxes vary greatly, from stereo to iPod to TV to greeting card, but this new kind of music is essentially the same. It is dead music. The music is dead in three ways: in its relation to time, place and person.

First, most of this music is recorded, which means that it occurred sometime in the past; quite literally it is no longer alive. Even when something is called a "live" broadcast, there is no way for the listener to know this, there is nothing to distinguish it from recorded music. For the listener, there is nothing more alive about it than music recorded years before.

Secondly, this new kind of music is made in a place that is different from the place of the listener. The music maker is in one place and the music listener is in another. Place is not common to both, it does not unite them, it does not give them a common ground. An essential link between maker and listener is missing. Placeless music therefore marks a lessening of human connection. A certain kind of unique "aliveness" is absent.

Finally, all this music that surrounds us in modern society—and there is a huge amount of it—is totally impersonal music. The makers of the music do not personally know the listeners and the listeners do not know the makers. The music is broadcast, that is, thrown out, to countless, perhaps millions, of unknown persons. Usually, of course, the listeners don't know each other either. They form an audience of anonymous persons. It is a strange kind of music this music that forms so few bonds with others. It's the music of an impersonal, lonely world.

Modern music, this dead music, is made possible by a kind of disembodiment. The music is taken from the bodies, the hands and mouths, of those that make it and then tele-communicated elsewhere. Makers and listeners can then be bodily removed from each other. The significance of this for Christian faith is, I believe, quite profound. We are, after all, embodied beings, a composite of body and soul. We are different from the angels, those beings of pure spirit.

As embodied beings we can be in only one place at one time and face to face with only certain others. This is a necessary limitation that makes possible the uniqueness and glory of the kind of creatures that we are. Furthermore, and most significantly, the central mystery of our faith is an embodiment, the Incarnation—the Word made flesh in Jesus, who suffered and died and rose from the dead in a resurrected body.

Modern music, as disembodied music, must therefore have an inevitable influence on how we experience ourselves, our very natures, and our faith. It promotes in subtle and powerful ways illusions of disincarnation and maybe even denial of the Incarnation. I am not proposing, however, that we smash our music technologies. Rather, I believe sober and careful thinking appropriate to our times is required. Perhaps reflections of this sort might lead us to a grateful enjoyment of the exquisite aliveness to person, place and moment that is possible when we gather together at Christ Church on Sunday mornings to pray and sing.

LIVING IN THE
VIRTUAL WORLD

I fear for my grandchildren. I wonder: What kind of world are they growing up in?

When I was their age, growing up in the 1950s, the world consisted of three classes of objects: other people, nature, and artifacts (man-made things). There was a solidness to this world. You could put your hands on it, taste it, smell it. Everything within it was graspable, whether it was friends or family; rocks, trees or dogs; cars, furniture or toys. This world was tangible.

That would change when I was 4 years old. A new kind of object entered my world, something unlike anything else.

My family got a television.

The TV was an artifact, but of an entirely unprecedented kind. Essentially, it was a machine that produced illusions. When I watched it in my living room, it made me feel that I was someplace else, in a different world but surrounded by objects as real and tangible as the ones I was familiar with. But I wasn't, of course. I was only seeing phantoms of a sort, illusions created by the projection of light onto a glass screen. I had entered a world entirely composed of two-dimensional, flickering images—the virtual world.

I had had this experience before with the few movies I had seen, but those were rare and the TV brought the experience into the home and made it a daily occurrence.

The influence of the virtual world on me and society at large would grow over the years. The high school I attended in the 1960's had large TVs in every homeroom. A wealthy alumnus had donated them to the school, believing that they would be an indispensable tool for education. They went largely unused, but the idea was out there. The virtual world would be the wave of the future.

And it has come to pass. Computer and digital technologies have enormously expanded the power to make and display the virtual world far beyond our old TVs. No longer confined to our living rooms, the glass screen's entrances into the virtual world are now present everywhere. You see them in every kind of building (schools, offices, libraries, restaurants, sporting arenas, hospitals, etc.), in vehicles that travel the ground, air, or sea; and people carry them around with them in their pockets or the palms of their hands. Screens are truly omnipresent.

So this then is the world in which my grandchildren are growing up, so different from the one I was introduced to. In this brave new world in which we wander, my fears for them and us center on three main questions:

• Do the habits of thinking, feeling and perceiving acquired in the virtual world stay with us when we leave it and re-enter the real world?

• Do we imperceptibly at some point begin to lose our ability to distinguish the virtual world from the real world?
• Is the real world being transformed into something more and more resembling the virtual world—ephemeral, insubstantial, endlessly manipulable?

In pondering these questions, I am reminded of an ancient warning about a certain kind of image-making: "They have eyes but cannot see and ears but cannot hear. And those who make them are like them, as are those who put their trust in them."

ON TIME

The theme for today's service is time, perspectives on time. Through stories, songs and reflections, we invite you to join us in thinking about how we experience time, what we understand it to be, and what meaning we find in it.

This theme has suggested itself to us by the fact that today begins Daylight Savings Time. By your timely presence here this morning, you have demonstrated a familiarity with this kind of time—you have dutifully turned your clocks one hour ahead. Perhaps then to begin with it might be good to bear in mind how we conceive of time when looking at a clock.

We take clocks for granted; they are so ubiquitous in modern life. But it wasn't always so. Historically the mechanical clock first made its appearance in the 14th century in the clock towers of major cities in Western Europe. They were crude devices, with only hour hands, and not very accurate. The domestic clock wouldn't come along until the end of the 16th century and principally in the homes of the wealthy. But the early clocks had initiated a radically new way of thinking about time—a way that has now conquered the entire world.

The clock introduced the notion of time as being measured by abstract, uniform units, dissociated from human experience or the natural world. Time became quantifiable, a purely mathematical conception.

Previously people had always marked time by changes in nature or in human events: the passage of the sun through the sky, which the sun dial traces; the changes of the seasons; work rhythms—harvest time; or cultural rhythms—festivals, feast time.

In this order of time, no two times are exactly the same. The setting sun is always different, each day is a bit longer or shorter than the next. Every birthday is unique, every Christmas different. There is regularity here, but it is pervaded with uniqueness.

There are no differences in clock time, except for numerical differences. As pure abstraction, everything but quantification is filtered out. An hour today is the same as an hour yesterday. Five minutes is five minutes, here or there. This is disembodied time, a formal, mental construct.

Lewis Mumford writes that the clock, not the steam engine, is the key machine of the modern industrial age. It also became a powerful new metaphor: the world started to look like a clock, including the organisms within it. The living organic world for the first time was examined as a mechanical device. You see this with the founders of modern philosophy in Hobbes and Descartes.

The new sense of power over time which clocks gave

has changed our language as well. We commonly speak of time as a commodity, something we can possess. We save time, spend time, lose time, waste time, use time, make time, find time, and keep time. With so many clocks and so much power over time, why do we always feel we have so little time? So little time for each other?

So this morning, while we live in a world of Eastern Standard Time and Daylight Savings Time, let us cherish these moments together, by being fully present to each other, and perhaps we can call this time First Parish Time.

V.

FROM THE ECONOMY
TO FRIENDSHIP

FROM THE ECONOMY
TO FRIENDSHIP
MY YEARS STUDYING IVAN ILLICH

One summer morning in 1973 Ivan lllich was conducting his seminar "Limits to Growth" in Cuernavaca, Mexico. He sat on a wall surrounding the veranda of the Casa Blanca, an old hacienda on the grounds of his alternative learning arrangement, the Center for Intercultural Documentation (CIDOC). I had positioned myself a little below and behind him on the stairs that led up to the veranda. As I sat there, not really following the conversation closely, I felt overcome by a turmoil of anger and contempt for this man.

For several weeks since my arrival at CIDOC, I had been trying to size up this controversial figure. Along with many others, I found him to be brilliant; his intellect was dazzling and formidable, like none I had ever encountered; he was charismatic, too. There was a remarkable presence and aliveness about him. But he was not just a man of ideas. What he had done at CIDOC was very different from any educational institution I was familiar with. It had little administration, no salaried staff, and no credits or degrees issued. Yet about the place there was a palpable air of

171

devotion to learning. Perhaps it was closer to the original idea of a university than more conventional counterparts.

Well, this was all fine and good, but still I wondered, What was its relevance to the poor? Was Illich really concerned about them? What was he proposing to do for those living in desperate conditions, or for those suffering under oppressive military regimes in Latin America? Was CIDOC anything more than a privileged enclosure?

After much thought and many conversations with other American students at CIDOC, I made up my mind. I came to the seminar that morning having concluded the night before that Illich was a phony, someone enmeshed in his own cleverness, a dangerous distraction from the pressing social concerns of the day. Yet I must have had some lingering doubts. How else to explain my presence on those steps and the intensity of my feelings?

As I watched Illich, I felt my anger grow with each word he spoke. And then a strange thing happened: He suddenly turned toward me. To see where I sat he had to turn quite far, but I was not sure whether he saw me because I was on the periphery of his vision; and he did not know me. I wondered, Had he sensed my anger? He continued speaking, all the while looking intensely at me, as if he really wanted me to understand what he was saying. I returned his gaze and although I did not understand a word he said, I felt the confusion of my thoughts and feelings inexplicably lifted from me. In those few moments I had the experience of intimately seeing this person, Ivan Illich, for the first time; I then knew he was someone

I could trust. But I would not have a direct conversation with him for many years to come.

I went to CIDOC at the age of twenty-three. I was entering law school that fall, but I did not know where that would take me. Like many other American students at CIDOC, I came with grave concerns about my own country. This was a time of much social turmoil and unrest in the United States. The Vietnam War lingered on; the Watergate hearings had just begun. Throughout Latin America, military dictatorships were in power due to United States' support. At home, protest was often met with official violence. Dissident groups—students, Blacks, farmworkers, prisoners, Native Americans—all had their casualties. Fresh in my mind were the events at Wounded Knee, Kent State, and Attica State Prison. It seemed to me at the time, as it did to many others, that violence was somehow inherent to American society.

Prior to my arrival at CIDOC, I had worked for a year as a laborer in factories: first in a carpet mill and then later in an automobile assembly plant. I needed to earn money, but I also wanted to be closer to the world of those I thought of then as being in the working-class, the blue-collar worker. My experiences in these factories left me thinking that a kind of violence was done to workers by mass production —to their spirit and sometimes to their bodies also; and this had something to do with the more overt kinds of violence so much in the news.

I went to CIDOC with a lot on my mind: How was I to make sense of my own country? How would I be able to live honorably in it? What kind of work could I find to do? I had decided that I would study law to work for social justice. I went to CIDOC primarily to learn Spanish (CIDOC was reported to have the best language school in Latin America). I figured that there were many Spanish-speaking people who could use a good lawyer. But I also wanted to sit in on some of the courses and lectures that seemed so interesting. Here was a place that addressed many of the questions that were most on my mind, where scholars and social activists from around the world came to discuss politics, economics, and social change. I hoped to gain some clarity in my thinking, and inspiration from those who were living out their ideals in their own societies.

For many of us at CIDOC—like myself, college-educated, middle-class, and socially concerned—Illich was not what we expected. He did not speak in the usual terms of radical politics; he did not talk much of class struggle, oppressor and oppressed, or movement politics. He even seemed to question our good intentions. He would not flatter our sense of moral superiority or romanticize those we considered disadvantaged in the United States (the poor in the United States consumed far more than the majority in the Third World could ever hope to, he pointed out). How radical were we? he seemed to ask. Were we wedded to the American way of life underneath our outward display of desire for change?

Prior to my exposure to Illich, all the politics I was familiar with were based on a common premise: Social justice was seen largely in terms of distributive justice. Most of the problems in society could be solved if its poorer segments were to receive a fairer share of the output of the industrial economy. If the bloated military budget were reduced, think of how much more would be available for better housing, education, jobs, and health care for the poor. Capitalists, Communists, and Socialists all had different ideas on how to bring about a fairer distribution of goods and services, but each took for granted an industrial economy, the industrial mode of production.

Illich challenged this. Turning the political debate inside out, he claimed that it is the industrial mode of production itself that is the source of our ills. Industrial growth does not liberate, rather it forces people into a new kind of serfdom. He argued that a life of dependency on mass-produced goods and services extinguishes the very conditions for a good life. And while some were beginning to be concerned with the overproduction of goods—the waste, pollution, and glut they create—Illich went much further. He criticized those more intangible commodities: services. What everyone looked on as an unquestioned benefit—education, health care, social services—Illich called harmful and disabling.

This was all very confusing to me at the time. What was I to make of Illich's startling, paradoxical aphorisms: schools stupify, cars paralyze, medicine sickens? When listening to him I often had the experience that it was as if I were learning a new language, and with it a new way of thinking and seeing. As with learning a language, I found it difficult and frustrating, and I wondered if I would ever understand it. But through it all, I had the sense that Illich was on to something, that he had an insight into a truth I did not want to miss. Perhaps he was a thinker who was able to slice through the Gordian knot of our modern dilemmas.

When I returned to the United States, I started law school and I did not meet Illich again until eleven years later. But I began a serious study of all he had written, and all I could find about him. I also began to test out his ideas in my own life.

One thing I had a lot of experience with at that time was educational institutions; most of my life had been spent in them—seventeen years by the time I began law school. The arguments of *Deschooling Society* made a lot of sense to me, my experience confirmed them. The book was also helpful. It gave me the courage to skip most of my classes the last year of law school, so that I could work as much as possible in a legal aid office, learning the skills of a practicing attorney.

After graduating I found a job with an older attorney in a small law firm in Waltham, Massachusetts. Within a year I moved to this city (I'm still there, in the same city and law office). I had read *Energy and Equity* and knew I did not want to be a commuter. I also wanted to know and be a part of the community where I worked; I wanted to be rooted in a place. Illich helped me to see this more clearly.

I began the practice of law in the hopes that I could use law as an instrument for social change. That some kind of radical change was needed seemed obvious to me at the time. In addition to Illich, I was reading several other perceptive critics of industrial society: Lewis Mumford, E.F. Schumacher, and Peter Maurin. Each in his own unique way showed the present system to be fundamentally flawed. Whether called industrialization, progress, modernity, growth, or development, this way could not but lead to more of the destructive results that were becoming so familiar: a growing gap between rich and poor, both within countries and among them; more degradation of the natural world—the earth becoming a global strip mine and dump; more dehumanizing work and addictive consumption of all kinds; the loss of traditional societies and cultures; increased anxiety and loneliness among the elites, and disorientation among the majority; finally, to keep it all together, a greater and more pervasive police and military presence.

How to find a way out of this mess? What was the alternative? While none of the authors whom I found most insightful had a blueprint, and each emphasized different things (e.g., Illich spoke of conviviality), there was a consensus among them about the general outlines of the desirable society. It would be smaller in scale, more decentralized, with fewer things, but things that are durable and repairable. It would be a society more in harmony with nature, with a close relationship between farm and city, and a better balance between work of the head and that of the hand; where mutual aid and self-sufficiency prevailed, and leisure enriched community life.

I had been particularly inspired by Peter Maurin's exhortation "build the new society in the shell of the old."

This was not a call for revolution in the usual sense, but a challenge to each person to live out in his own life the change he wished to see in society. I thought this personal, grassroots approach to social change could fit in with the practice of law. I would be working directly with people, in face-to-face relationships, helping them with a specific concern. In this way I hoped to get to know people better and become part of my community. I especially thought of *Tools for Conviviality*, in which Illich had spoken of law as a potentially convivial tool, that it could be a means for challenging and even stopping industrial growth. Perhaps I could find ways to do this and foster alternatives.

Over the course of the next five years or so I was immersed in learning the ropes of a legal practice. The kind of law we did, general practice, put me in touch with the way law affects the lives of the great majority of people: through wills, divorce, criminal defense, disability claims, auto accidents, buying and selling homes, tenant and consumer cases. While I received a lot of satisfaction from seeing a good result achieved for individual clients, I began to be troubled by something: A good result might benefit someone in the short term, but I did not see it having any larger effect. I saw that the ordinary practice of law did not work so much to make society more just but rather kept things as they were, and running smoothly. I also found that the activities that gave me the most satisfaction—involvement with a local nuclear weapons freeze group, a campaign that stopped the building of a road through a park, and advising homeschoolers—had little to do with the everyday work in my law office. As I became more frustrated, I began to get a better grasp of something Illich had been pointing out for a long time.

Alone among the critics of industrialism, Illich began his analysis with a focus on the service sector. Initially starting with the Church, he moved on to education and then medicine. Each time with increasing depth and clarity he showed how services are as much a product of an industrial mode of production as goods. And most surprisingly, he argued that just as the overproduction of goods has unwanted side effects harmful to society, so too do services. Both result in something he called "paradoxical counter-productivity," the puzzling phenomenon of an institution or agency frustrating the very purpose it was originally designed to accomplish. For example, we see this with schools producing bored, passive, and dulled students; or with medical practices that sicken people and foster unhealthy environments and lifestyles.

I really did not understand this until I had been practicing law for a while. Besides being a licensed professional (a full-fledged member of the service economy), I was put right in the middle of the social services world by the kind of legal work I did. Regularly, I dealt with the great social service systems of modern society and their agents: social workers, doctors, counselors, police, teachers, lawyers, and administrators of all kinds. As I gained familiarity with how these systems function, I began to notice certain characteristics.

First, each system operates as a business (as does my

law practice), which generates income and prestige for those working in it. Despite the lofty ideals upon which each system was founded, rarely would anyone act in a way that threatens one's position and security within the system. Secondly, just as with any business, social service systems need markets. In this case, their customers are the potential clients for the services they provide. Through training and institutional momentum, and often with the best of intentions, service providers see people as being in need of their services. Police find more people to arrest and others to protect. Social workers classify more families and children "at risk." Doctors diagnose more patients in need of expensive tests and treatments. All of this is good for business. It is also insidious since service systems take away from people what they could do on their own, or for each other—or do without—and replace it with a dependency relationship. People lose the capacity to heal, learn, grieve, console, and resolve disputes without professional assistance. In this way, the more people lose self-reliance and independence, the better for the economy.

After a while, I saw the joke. When people asked me, "How's work going?" I would answer, "Never been better. Families are falling apart, so there is plenty of divorce and juvenile delinquency; arrests are up, so I have a lot of criminal trials; auto accidents and injuries at work are high, so my personal injury caseload is huge. Business is good." In a strange way, all of us in the service economy are feeding off social decay, a kind of cannibalizing of society.

In *Shadow Work* and *Gender*, Illich explains this phenomenon as being the natural outcome of the "disembedding of the economy." Examining the historical origins of modern society, Illich points out in these two works that all previous societies limited economic activity by weaving it tightly into the social fabric. Embedded in an intricate pattern of complementary social relations, purely economic behavior could not emerge. Once released from social restraints by modernization, however, a disembedded economy proved to be a relentless force, one that dismantled traditional societies piece by piece. The innumerable and varied ways in which people got by and got along were replaced with a life of dependency on commodities (both goods and services) and wage labor. We don't so much have a society any longer, Illich argued, as an economy,

As I came to understand this, I found myself in a quandary. If all economic activity has a corrosive effect on society, how is one to act ethically? Modern life is tightly bound up by market relations. Illich contrasted the economic with premodern ways of living he called subsistence or the vernacular. He proposed a "modern subsistence" as an alternative to economics as a way to "break the cash nexus." But, I wondered, where were the examples? I knew that many of those who had attempted to live outside the economy in the back-to-the-land movement failed. I admired the success of the Amish but felt no calling to their way; further, I had friends and family I did not want to leave. Also, being married, I could not just force my ideas on my wife. What could I do? Was there no way out?

At about the time when I was grappling most with

these questions, and feeling a kind of despair at not being able to come up with answers, I found in the morning's mail a flyer with Illich's picture on the cover. The brochure, which had been sent to me due to my work with home-schoolers, announced the Maine Summer Institute, a weeklong conference featuring Illich and several of his colleagues. Organized by a friend of his and funded by the University of Maine, it focused on the theme "The History of Economic Man." At the conference I met Illich personally for the first time and got to see a little of how he lived his life. This was July, 1984.

Held in a stately private school during its summer recess, the meeting had about it the invigorating air of CIDOC. All participants, including speakers, were housed in dormitories and ate their meals together in the cafeteria; it made me think of some kind of gypsy camp. Here were these wayfarers, Illich and his friends (he seemed to have friends, not disciples) coming together from far-off places, pitching their tents and having a kind of party. There were jokes about "Ivan's flying circus" and the "floating crap game." The joy Illich felt in the presence of his friends was evident, as was theirs in him, all of which was heightened by the transitoriness of the whole event.

And then there were the conversations; most took place in the cafeteria after meals. They were lively and intense, a heady intellectual experience for me, and they never seemed to end, often running late into the night. I discovered that these discussions were really the heart of the conference, the formal presentations being a nice

182

complement to them.

I learned that CIDOC had closed in 1976 and Illich was now teaching at a university in Germany. This gave me pause. Here was the world's foremost critic of education and high-speed transportation teaching at a university and flying around in jets. What was I to make of that? Was Illich a hypocrite? Surprisingly, it was through this example of his life that I would get an answer to my dilemma and find an insight into a way of living in the midst of the industrial economy.

No, Illich was not a hypocrite. Nor was he a purist or puritan; he was dealing with the realities of his life. The sad fact is that there is no escape from the industrial economy; there is no way to live entirely outside it. How could one avoid riding in cars, for example, when the social and physical landscape has been reconstructed around their use? Illich seemed to say, "Let's face up to it; let's not delude ourselves about the humiliating conditions under which we live—we are trapped in many ways. Know what this way of life is doing to you, to others, and to nature. Don't be seduced by the advertisers. Have the courage to recognize the ugliness of modern life—and to suffer it."

On the other hand, Illich was not counseling despair or resignation. He believed that there were ways in which one could withdraw, at least to some degree, from the economy, taking into account the unique circumstances of each one's life. This was a messy business; there were no hard and fast rules, nor occasions for self-righteousness. But acts of resistance and refusal were possible. Illich himself

183

lived a very modest and disciplined life; he set a limit on how much money he would earn. He found a way to live on the margins of university life—he did not get involved with grading students, attending committee meetings, or chasing tenure. Most important, Illich used his involvement with the economy to foster its opposite: the vernacular or convivial life. With his own money, he supported friends who were doing good work. He used his lectures and discussions with students to further his critique of industrial society, and explore ways out of it. He also seemed to have a nose for finding the niches and cracks in the established order, places where he could foster, with friends and students, a certain *joie de vivre*, a sense of freedom and relatedness.

I came home from Maine renewed; I realized that I did not have to quit my job—I could simply work at it less. I soon began a four-day week, which freed me up to read and study more, and become more active in my community. I did not have to get rid of my car, but I could ride my bicycle to work. 1 knew I would not be self-sufficient in growing food, but I could do composting and enlarge our vegetable garden. Later, when we had children, it was an easy decision not to put them in school. I also began to see my legal work in a new light. I knew it would not lead to social change (with the possible exception of homeschooling cases), but my clients' concerns were real, they were entangled in a morass of legal and social systems. Perhaps I could be an experienced guide for them through these thickets.

Starting in 1988, I began to visit Illich each year, often

more than once a year. Most of these meetings were at Pennsylvania State University, where he taught in the fall, but there were many other places as well, including his home in Mexico. No matter the setting, certain common features became familiar to me. There was always a house with rooms for guests, who came from near and far. There were the simple but good meals together, served with wine and embellished with flowers on the table; and, of course, the conversations. Many times a "living room" conference took place, with people coming together for several days to examine and discuss a particular topic. Illich was always the gracious host, attentive to all his guests, taking great pleasure in such humble signs of affection as making a cup of tea for someone.

For me, these visits became a kind of retreat, a way to get my bearings in the brave new world being fashioned in the 1980's and 1990's by the global economy and high technology. I came home from these trips and asked myself if I could organize in my life something like the households I visited. Could I somehow foster that kind of aliveness—that kind of presence to person, place, and moment. It was such a contrast to a society that seemed to grow ever duller and more homogenized as the allurements for staring into a glass screen became evermore powerful.

The key to the atmosphere of hospitality and celebration I experienced during my visits was clearly Illich's friendships with his guests. He was a most devoted friend to all of us; someone who had cultivated the art of friendship to a high degree—and the habits of the heart that make friendship possible. But his was not an exclusive kind of friendship. He would remind us that the friendship between two people must always be open to a third—the stranger who surprises us with a knock at the door.

The more I came to know Illich personally, the more I would see that friendship was the very center of his life and work. While he never wrote an essay or treatise explicitly on the subject, friendship is a theme that consistently appears in his writing, a connecting thread through all his books. I eventually concluded that the best way to understand Illich's work is a detailed study of the myriad and varied barriers to friendship that exist in modern life. The kinds of withdrawal and resistance he encouraged, what he later would call *ascesis*, was a new kind of asceticism, practices that are a necessary condition for friendship to flower in our modern deserts.

It is all so startling really, that I continue to be amazed. No one I know has seen so deeply as Illich the darkness of our times, no one has examined with such an unflinching eye the enormity of the evil we face. Yet he rests his hope on such a humble, fragile, one might easily say foolish, task: the simple but arduous one of being present to this person who stands in front of me. Then, I need to define myself and act in terms of the bonds that connect me to others—my family, friends, neighbors, and whoever may stumble unexpectedly into my life. Perhaps Illich is foolish, at least in the opinion of many, but there is something about him that assures me he is right—his joyfulness.

When I think back over the years since I sat on those

steps of the Casa Blanca, I am filled with an overwhelming sense of gratitude. How I have been blessed! How could I ever repay Ivan Illich for all he has given me? But I know he would want me to be more precise with my language. Friendship does not lend itself to an accounting, to economics. The only way I can hope to show my gratitude is to strive to be for others the kind of friend Ivan Illich has been to me.

—Waltham, Massachusetts

NOTES

Ivan Illich, *Deschooling Society* (New York: Harper and Row, 1971).

Ivan Illich, *Energy and Equity* (New York: Harper and Row, 1974).

Lewis Mumford, *Myth of the Machine*, 2 vols. (New York: Harcourt Brace, 1974); E. F. Schumacher, *Small is Beautiful* (New York: Harper and Row, 1989); and Peter Maurin, *Easy Essays* (Chicago: Franciscan Herald Press, 1984).

Ivan Illich, *Tools for Conviviality* (New York: Harper and Row, 1973).

See Geoffrey B. Gneuhs, "Peter Maurin's Personalist Democracy," in Patrick G. Coy, ed., *A Revolution of the Heart: Essays on the Catholic Worker* (Philadelphia: Temple University Press, 1988), pp. 47–68.

Illich, *Tools for Conviviality*, pp. 99–107.

Ivan Illich, *Shadow Work* (London: Marion Boyars, 1981), pp. 99–116; and Ivan Illich, *Gender* (New York: Pantheon, 1982), p. 12.

Now most of my clients are Guatemalan immigrants.

AFTERWORD

Many activists and writers say to themselves, "I should write a column for the local paper." Most of us never get around to it. But Gene Burkart got around to doing most things that mattered.

In addition to writing numerous letters and columns for the Waltham *News Tribune* and other publications, he was involved in Waltham Concerned Citizens, a peace group; GROW (Green Rows of Waltham) community garden; various religious congregations; as well as numerous other activities in Waltham. He truly walked the walk along with talking the talk, whether that meant biking to work, providing legal services to the poor and disenfranchised, homeschooling his children, housing those in need, or standing outside Raytheon headquarters with a sign calling for a nuclear weapons freeze.

He was Waltham's Dorothy Day, our Gandhi, our Thoreau and Howard Zinn, our conscience, hero, friend. The world and our community are a much poorer place for the loss of this humane, thoughtful, thought-provoking man, who lived his life with such profound intention. As one commentator on the *News Tribune* website mentioned, "For those who never met him, I'd like you to know that even if you disagreed with him politically, you would have found him to be an exceptionally kind, thoughtful man."

Re-reading these pieces—and reading some of them

for the first time—I'm struck by the breadth of Gene's knowledge, from history to economics, theology to mythology, literature to sociology, and how he wove those together. Sometimes he would write two versions of the same article or speech for different venues It is impressive to compare the two and see how Gene subtly shaped them for his separate audiences. No matter what, he was never condescending. He wore his learning lightly and shared his thoughts patiently and logically. His writing had an engaging conversational quality, though, as I examine it again, I see poetry alongside the philosophy.

He returned again and again, eloquently and urgently, to the topic of the bombings of Hiroshima and Nagasaki, an historical and theological theme for him but one that was also personal: he was born at Los Alamos, where his father was stationed and had worked on the atomic bomb. In August, 2012, even as he struggled against the effects of cancer that would take him days later, Gene wrote a column about Hiroshima and attended Waltham Concerned Citizens' annual Hiroshima vigil, his final act of witness.

Gene called his newspaper column "Second Thoughts." I always found this odd, since there is no one I know who had less reason to have second thoughts. He lived his life with profound intention and thoughtfulness. May these writings inspire all of us to live as fully and meaningfully as Gene.

Jennifer Rose
March, 2014

You can order additional copies of this book at
www.amazon.com.

About the Author

Eugene J. Burkart (1950–2012) was born in Los Alamos, New Mexico. After attending Holy Cross College, he earned a law degree from Suffolk Law School in 1976. A lawyer by trade, Burkart was a frequent newspaper columnist, and active in many social and religious causes in his adopted hometown of Waltham, Massachusetts. He is survived by his wife Sue, two sons, and three grandchildren.